Lieutenant Presley Neville O'Bannon, USMC, 1801-1807
Painting by Colonel Donald L. Dickson, USMCR, 1960. The original oil painting hangs
in O'Bannon Hall, Basic School, Marine Corps Schools, Quantico, Virginia.
Courtesy U.S. Marine Corps Museum

Valiant Virginian

Story of
Presley Neville O'Bannon
1776-1850

First Lieutenant U.S. Marine Corps
1801-1807

by
Trudy J. Sundberg and John K. Gott

To Which is Added

The O'Bannon Family

Descendants of
Bryan O'Bannon of
Ireland and Fauquier County, Virginia

by
John K. Gott

HERITAGE BOOKS
2007

HERITAGE BOOKS
AN IMPRINT OF HERITAGE BOOKS, INC.

Books, CDs, and more—Worldwide

For our listing of thousands of titles see our website
at
www.HeritageBooks.com

Published 2007 by
HERITAGE BOOKS, INC.
Publishing Division
65 East Main Street
Westminster, Maryland 21157-5026

International Standard Book Number: 978-0-7884-0067-3

CONTENTS

VALIANT VIRGINIAN

STORY OF

PRESLEY NEVILLE O'BANNON

1776 - 1850

FIRST LIEUTENANT U. S. MARINE CORPS

HERO OF THE TRIPOLITAN WAR

1801 -- 1807

by

Trudy J. Sundberg

and

John K. Gott

To John Sundberg
     -Trudy

and

To Lou B. O'Bannon
     -John Gott

Table of Contents

"Posterity! You will never know how much it cost the present generation to preserve your freedom. I hope you will make good use of it."

John Adams

SYNOPSIS

What makes a good adventure story? Pirates can always be relied upon for excitement and daring deeds. Turks and Arabs are often the source of exotic interest. Sun-scorched deserts are ideal places for dreadful things to happen. Handsome, young heroes fighting in hand-to-hand combat make the best battle scenes. International intrigue adds to a suspenseful take and the United States Marines can be expected to come through any battle whatever the odds.

The above examples of character, setting and conflict might find their way into a dozen films and novels. Rarely, however, would a writer try to include all of these dramatic aspects into one book or screenplay, least of all have the audacity to present them as true, historical information.

Nevertheless, there is a true story about a handsome, young Virginian, Presley Neville O'Bannon, which involved the Barbary Coast in Africa, a 700-mile march across the sinister Barca Desert in Libya, and the strange Tripolitan War. What's more, the story has important historical significance, because it is about the first man to raise the American flag, in victory, over the walls of a fortress in the Old World. It is a story relating to the words in the Marine Hymn, "From the Halls of Montezuma to the shores of Tripoli..." It is a story of extraordinary heroism even in military annals where danger and terror are often part of the daily routine.

Artists, historians and Hollywood have well preserved the flamboyant feats of Stephen Decatur and United States' sea battles with pirates and corsairs during this period of history in the early 1800's. Unfortunately, they have neglected to a large extent the decisive battle that was fought by a raggle-taggle foreign legion on a sizzling, sandy desert without adequate experience, supplies, assistance, government support or trained soldiers.

This then is the story of Presley Neville O'Bannon, one of America's all-but-forgotten heroes, who helped in putting an end to piracy on the Barbary Coast and in stopping the Tripolitan War.

CHAPTER ONE

AN ABOMINABLE SITUATION

"O'Bannon stands for the highest type of patriotic and hard-fighting officer of the Marine Corps and his career typifies most perfectly what is expected of a Marine in times of great national stress."

Thomas Holcomb
Commandant, U.S.M.C.

Individually and collectively, the names George Washington, Thomas Jefferson, Patrick Henry, James Madison, John Marshall and George Mason strike a resonant chord in the hearts of freedom-loving people around the world. Individually, each was a titan, whose vision, imagination, energy and wisdom were vital in the creation of our unique nation. Collectively, they continue to evoke our awe.

No people in the world can boast of more extraordinary men living in close proximity of time and territory than these six remarkable individuals, who were born within a time span of three decades (1725-1755) and within a radius of one hundred miles.

From this same fecund, Virginia soil, another unusual young man claimed his origin during the early struggling years of this country's history. Presley Neville O'Bannon was born to William and Nancy (Neville) O'Bannon in the cataclysmic year of 1776.

The greater part of Virginia at this time was still wilderness. In the back country where O'Bannon grew up, life was rugged. Women and men worked from dawn to dark, thorns were used for pins, cloth was homespun, pioneers hunted for game, fish and bear meat and almost every man and young boy became proficient with his rifle. Living a rigorous outdoor life amidst the perils of the forest and the elements of nature, backwoodsmen developed self-reliance, versatility, strength of character, initiative and a sense of personal testing.

Thomas Jefferson described Northern Virginia society as aristocratic, pompous and indolent. Very little attention was given to public education. Except for the sons of wealthy plantation owners, who were sent to English schools, few boys and almost no girls were taught to read and write before the 1800's.

However, in spite of the wealth, education and prestige of the aristocratic families of Virginia, it was the backwoodsmen (many originally from uncommonly well-educated English families) who profoundly influenced the social, political, industrial, literary, legal and military history of the United States for generations.

At the age of 25 when most young men in Virginia were establishing their own homes, raising tobacco or perhaps following George Washington's footsteps by learning surveying, young O'Bannon left his boyhood days in Virginia behind and accepted a commission as a second lieutenant in the United States Marine Corps on 18 January 1801.

One year later Lt. O'Bannon was assigned to duty in New York on board the frigate Adams which was being made seaworthy in the East River for a cruise to the Mediterranean. Lt. O'Bannon very faithfully reported to his commanding officer, the Commandant of the Marine Corps, Lt. Col. William W. Burrows. The existing letters to Lt. Col. Burrows indicate a very warm, personal friendship existing between the two gentlemen. Unlike most official reports, he never failed to interject a greeting for Mrs. Burrows and the Commandant's family:

> My best respects to Mrs. Burrows & family & the Officers at HdQuarters.

When Lt. Col. Franklin Wharton became the Commandant in 1804 the letters ceased or have been lost. Lt. O'Bannon kept busy during the time he was in New York chasing deserters, keeping the men in his detachment well clothed, seeing to their medical needs and recruiting:

> I hope ere this, you have rec'd my Pay Roll - I come on slowly Recruiting, because I refuse to take Irishmen.

During his assignment at the Marine Barracks in Washington he made many friends among the commissioned staff and one cannot but feel a bit of homesickness when he wrote Col. Burrows on 12 December 1801:

> I should have no objections to have made one of your party at Lieut. Rankin's Wedding, and not the smallest objection to have been one of the party at the Punch- Drinking.

On 23 April 1802 Lt. O'Bannon reported to Lt. Col. Burrows that

> The Muskets belonging to my Detachment are (some of them) of the worst kind, as well as a deficiency of five - which makes it necessary for me to request that you will forward an Order, on the Navy Agent, which will enable me to get them.

Lt. Col. Burrows noted at the bottom of the letter

> Please forward an Order for Eight Muskets.

In the same month of the same year that O'Bannon joined the Marines another notable citizen of Fauquier County was launched into an important role in history. This Virginian was the honorable John Marshall, who at the age of 45 was nominated by President John Adams on 31 January 1801, as the fourth Chief Justice of the United States. While Chief Justice Marshall was using his brilliant legal mind to establish the right of nations under international law, by a strange coincidence of fate, the other native from Fauquier County, Second Lieutenant O'Bannon, was fighting on the Northern Coast of Africa with a musket for the same cause. The Fauquier County homes of these two illustrious Virginians were approximately three miles apart. History does not tell us, but it is interesting to conjecture that Presley N. O'Bannon received his education from the Rev. James Thomson, Rector of Leeds Parish, who was Marshall's tutor. O'Bannon received a good education if his letters and handwriting are any indication. Seldom did he use incorrect grammar and in comparison with Chief Justice Marshall's handwriting, O'Bannon was superior!

Many United States citizens during the days of Thomas Jefferson had never heard of such faraway places as Morocco, Algiers, Tunis and Tripoli. Furthermore, Americans were simply not interested in the demands and dealings of these remote rulers called Bashaws, Pashaws, Beys and Deys. The prevailing attitude of the country at that time was one of isolationism, non-interventionism and economy in military spending. O'Bannon mentioned this economy, which he felt to be foolhardy in the following letter:

Frigate Adams
May 15, 1802

Col. Burrows
Sir

At the request of Lieut. Thompson, Gersham Weldon has been paid up to the 30th Inst. and Discharged. - and as the time of Wm. Young expires tomorrow, - I have taken the liberty of Discharging him toDay, in order to meet the approbation of Republican economy, as by that is affected, part of the Savings intended by the Midnight motion of Gen'l. Mason ...

The entire Marine Corps in 1803, after Tripoli and Morocco had declared war on the United States, consisted of but 26 officers and 453 men, plus the Commandant in Washington and three staff officers at Headquarters who also performed line duty at the Washington barracks. There were only nine officers and 216 men in the Mediterranean in spite of the gravity of the situation and the actual threat to the United States' security.

Lt. O'Bannon was on duty at Marine Barracks, Navy Yard, New York from June 1801 to January 1802. He was on board the frigate Adams, at the navy Yard preparing for sea duty from January to June 1802. While stationed in New York, he took the opportunity to become a Freemason. He petitioned and became a member of St. Andrews Lodge No. 3, F&AM, taking all three degrees between 1 January and 13 May 1802. The Adams sailed for the Meditterranean in June 1802.

Although it might have come as a surprise to Captain William O'Bannon and his wife Nancy that their son Presley was sailing from New York to the Mediterranean on the frigate Adams on 10 June 1802, the orders were exactly what Lt. O'Bannon had anticipated. Lt. O'Bannon's letters indicate great excitement at the prospects of the cruise to the Mediterranean and his pleasure of being on board the Adams under the command of Captain Hugh G. Campbell. The voyage, except for a minor incident navigating around rocks off the coast of North Africa, and a clash of personalities between Captain Campbell and the First Lieutenant Isaac Hull, was uneventful. Upon reaching Gibraltar Bay on 15 December 1802 he was very prompt to write Col. Burrows of the clash:

... I am not a little pleased at having it in my power to inform you that Cap't. Campbell's Conduct towards me has been of a very different nature since my letter to you on that head. I was one of those whom Cap't. Campbell thot.

proper to treat with disrespect – (as I thought) – therefore decided it not amiss to mention it to you, and treat it as it deserved here, and this I done in a manner which my Station demanded, Since which there has remain'd a perfect understanding, and bids fair to remain so during the Cruize – in a word, I now have the Command of the Marines, which at that time was not the case, and which was the cause of difference.

This dispute, tho of a silent kind, was truly unpleasant to me, particularly as I know your respect for that Gent. – and permit me to assure you that your friendship has considerable weight with me – and together with my determination to cultivate and maintain the most perfect harmony, there remains very little doubt of a good understanding in future.

In the same letter he reported to his commanding officer of a duel and a brief mention of the real reason for the Navy's presence in the Mediterranean at this time; with a comment of his thoughts on taking a ship (even though an enemy ship) in a neutral port.

You have no doubt, ere this heard of the unfortunate fate of Capt McKnight, if not I have it not in my power to inform you further than he fell in a Duel with Lieut. Lawson of the same Frigate in or near the Town of Leghorn.

I ever Contended we had no right to make a prize of the Tripolitan Ship in this port and claimed by the Emperor of Morocco, but how far I was Correct I wont say – but this I know, that she has given up all pretentions of leaving this with her present pass ports, and is actually laid up in Ordinary[1] again, with only 3 or 4 men on Board –

The Adams had dropped anchor at Gibraltar under orders to keep the Tripolitan warship Meshuda, which had been blockaded there, under surveillance. According to a letter from Captain Campbell, written to Lieutenant Colonel, Commandant Burrows, 16 December 1802, O'Bannon managed to pass the time pleasantly at Gibraltar. "O'Bannon, one of the happiest fellows living, ... has just returned from spending the Evening with a Brilliant Circle of Spanish Ladys," Campbell wrote, "and by way of Consolation for the loss of their company, Philosophy and the fiddle is called to his aid; on the latter he is now playing Hogs in the Cornfield.'"

In spite of apathy and inadequate information at home, O'Bannon and his fellow shipmates were well informed on the nefarious system whereby all European countries, as well as the United States, directly or indirectly, went along with the demands of the Barbary Corsairs insisting on tribute in some form or another. Although the Tripolitan War has been recorded as the four year period between 1801 and 1805, terrorizing by the piratical state of Barbary had begun as early as the American Revolution and tributes amounting to millions of dollars were paid between 1785 and 1802.

Treaties with Morocco, Algiers, Tunis and Tripoli (the Barbary States) and big pay-offs kept a dishonorable peace for many years. But the corrupt system of tributes, like blackmail, was rapacious and never enough. Strangely enough, the only Americans who felt this shame and

---

[1] "Moth balls" is the term used today.

dishonor were those who had to suffer humiliation by laying gifts at the feet of the rulers and chieftains, by having to kiss their bejeweled hands, by being kept prisoners in dungeons and by being treated as captured slaves.

Even President John Adams (1797-1801), known as a man of dignity, intelligence and pride, was guilty of obsequious behavior in his relationship with the ruler of Tunisia. In a letter to the Tunisian chieftain he wrote: "To the most Illustrious and most Magnificent Prince, the Bey, who commands the Odgias of Tunic, the abode of happiness, and the most honored Ibrahim Dey and Soliman, Aga of the Janisaries and Chief of the Divan of all the Elders of the Odgias."

For over seventeen years the United States, in addition to paying millions of dollars in tribute, lavished the "barbarian" rulers with diamond decorated muskets, gold mounted pistols, gold snuffboxes and watches, "superfine cloth of different colours," fieldpieces, small arms, gunpowder, gun carriages, naval stores, diamond rings, a 36-gun ship the Cresent, the Hamdullah, the brig Sophia, two schooners, money for yearly peace, money for "perpetual peace," money for relief of prisoners, money for renewal of treaties and money to ransom the crew of the Franklin.

No one can quarrel with the altruistic and humanitarian desire of the American people and their leaders for wanting peace and friendly trade with the people of the world. Outright war with the Barbary States evolved, not because the United States could not bear the abject humiliation, but because their "presents" never seemed to buy the protection, free intercourse and friendly relations they had anticipated. Dissention began to grow in the United States with the memorable slogan, "Millions for defense but not one cent for tribute." Newspapers such as "The Museum & Washington & Georgetown Advertiser" carried an article on 11 March 1801, quoting Captain William Bainbridge as saying, "I hope I may never again be sent to Algiers with tribute, unless I am authorized to deliver it from the mouth of our cannon."

The capture of the Tripolitan polacres Tripoli by the Enterprise on August 1, 1801, with no American casualties and heavy losses by the Tripolitans caused considerable excitement in America. The marines were elated with their part in the conquest. Second Lieutenant Presley N. O'Bannon wrote his Commandant that he had "noticed with pleasure the credit which the Marines did themselves."

This increased anxiety, awareness and concern about ransoms, piracy and an uncertain peace were revealed in President Jefferson's speech to Congress on September 9, 1801, when he said, "We consented to give a price for friendship which would properly have been requited with our own. So long as we have been met with moderation and good faith we have preferred this means of peace, rather than seek it by our own strength. At length, however, the inadmissible demands of the Bey of Tripoli, and our own determination to owe to our own energies and not to dishonorable condescensions the protection of our rights to navigate the ocean freely, have induced us to send a squadron into the Mediterranean for the protection against the Bey of Tripoli."

During the two years before O'Bannon arrived in Tripoli, the Mediterranean "pot" had been boiling steadily. Algiers was smugly complacent about her $1,000,000 treaty; Tunisia was disgruntled and explosive; Morocco's mood was increasingly arrogant and Tripoli, believing she had made a bad bargain, hurled more threats and insults at the United States. Of the querulous lot, Tripoli was the most obdurate and unreasonable. As a result America was forced to arm, against her will, not to dominate the world, not to acquire new territory, not to gain power or glory, but simply to combat a rotten system of piracy that dominated Europe and threatened American citizens, commerce and goods.

Lt. O'Bannon's sense of duty, military bearing, patriotism and steady nerves in combat (that he was soon to display) could be attributed partly to the fact that he was fully aware of the situation along the north African Coast before his ship anchored off Tripoli and that he was also cognizant of the dangerous missions he would be involved in by joining the Marine Corps during such troubled times. By the time O'Bannon had been promoted to first lieutenant on October 15, 1802, the Bashaw of Tripoli had declared war against the United States by cutting down the flagstaff on the American Consulate. Still the United States did not retaliate by declaring war.

While O'Bannon was on the Adams, the Enterprise captured the Tripolitan polacre Tripoli, the navy and the marines continued to play the frustrating game of fighting Corsairs with one hand and offering them gifts with the other, and an Act of Congress in 1802 authorized the President to "subdue, seize and make prizes of the vessels of the Bey of Tripoli" and to do anything that "the state of war will justify." Six frigates and the schooner Enterprise arrived in the Mediterranean maelstrom between February and September.

Early in April of 1803 the U.S.S. Adams, with O'Bannon the only Marine officer on board, escorted a convoy of merchantmen to Malta by way of Leghorn, and about a month later joined Commodore Morris's squadron which was blockading Tripoli.

The first real action Lt. O'Bannon experienced at sea took place on the night of June 1, 1803, when the frigate Adams with the schooner Enterprise and the frigate New York sent fifty men in boats to burn Tripolitan vessels unloading grain in a small bay near Tripoli. The ships covered the attack and also fired on the shore defenses. "The Adams threw her shot excellently well," wrote Midshipman Henry Wadsworth on the New York. "Whenever three or four were seen running together, we would throw a twelve-pounder and, if they were not cut down, the sand would so cover them that, for a minute, you could not see them till at last the headmost one would make his appearance, followed by the others making haste for the first place of safety. T'was good sport I must confess," he continued, "Yet they might with justice join the Frogs in the Fable and say what is pleasure to you is death for us."

Unfortunately, the blockage and sporadic attacks had no effect on the Bashaw of Tripoli. The Adams was dispatched to Tunis with Consul James L. Cathcart, and then returned to Gibraltar. Because the Adams was ordered to return to the United States with Commodore R. V. Morris, O'Bannon was ordered to the President, the flagship of Commodore Samuel

Barron, who was to assume Commodore Edward Preble's assignment. As fate would have it, Lt. O'Bannon did not take part in the attacks on Tripoli and the encounter with Tripolitan gunboats there. Nor is his role in history involved in the daring burning of the Philadelphia. The story is by now well known and familiar about the Philadelphia, under the command of Captain William Bainbridge, which had run aground in Tripoli's harbor and had been captured with her crew. With the Philadelphia the Tripolitans had a potentially larger fleet than Prebles. Lt. Stephen Decatur with about 70 volunteers, entered the harbor at night in a captured Tripolitan ketch, appropriately renamed Intrepid, and sailed into the lion's jaws, into the midst of the Bashaw's fleet and the guns of the forts. Wearing Maltese attire, Decatur and a few other, stood on the deck. The remaining crew members lay breathlessly waiting. Decatur's Maltese pilot requested permission to tie up alongside the Philadelphia because of storm damage. At that point an alert Tripolitan screamed "Americanos," and the battle was on.

Decatur's Intrepid detachment scrambled up over the frigate's bulwarks. Fighting close and swift, they used cutlass, dirk and sword to rout the enemy. With remarkable speed and precision the Americans placed combustibles throughout the Philadelphia and escaped into the Intrepid as flames consumed the rigging. Against all odds, the ketch somehow escaped the shots from 100 guns surrounding the harbor without the loss of a man. The famous British hero, Admiral Lord Nelson, called this the "most bold and daring act of the age." In the eyes of some historians, the statement would be more correct if he had said, "the most bold and daring act of the age at sea." For the world had yet to learn of the incredible capture of Derna and of Lt. Presley N. O'Bannon's "bold and daring acts" in this military drama.

At Malta on October 23, 1804, the detachment of forty-nine Marines commanded by Captain Anthony Gale and Lieutenant O'Bannon were transferred to the Constitution from the President. The beginning of O'Bannon's real adventure began rather indirectly and inauspiciously three days later when he was ordered to the brig Argus commanded by Lt. Isaac Hull. Secret orders had been issued to Hull by Commodore Barron to transport a man named William Eaton to Alexandria, Egypt. It is possible that the chance meeting of O'Bannon and Eaton changed the course of history. At any rate, it is a fact that their combined talents on a dangerous expedition turned the tables of whole kingdoms and helped to establish the prestige, resourcefulness and power of a fledgling republic in the eyes of the world.

First of all, it is strange that fate ever brought this middle-aged New Englander and this young Southern officer together: Eaton, twelve years older than O'Bannon was born in Connecticut; O'Bannon was born in Virginia; Eaton attended Dartmouth College; O'Bannon never enrolled in college; Eaton ran away from home at sixteen to join the state militia; O'Bannon bid a fond farewell to his family to join the Marines at the age of twenty-five. Their personalities and character traits also differed as much as their backgrounds. Eaton served in the Revolutionary War and then under General "Mad Anthony" Wayne fighting against Ohio Indians. Yet his army record was smudged by reports of bad conduct and insubordination. Eaton was blustery, restless, arrogant, audacious and stubborn. O'Bannon was not a "glory hound" but a comely, affable, resourceful, well-disciplined, dependable, exemplary Marine officer.

The web of fate continued to weave intricate patterns six years later when William Eaton was a key witness in Aaron Burr's treason trial with Chief Justice John Marshall presiding.

CHAPTER TWO

COMPLICATIONS, SUSPICION AND INTRIGUE

"We must either bribe their avarice or chastise their audacity. Giving only increases their avidity for more .. It is devoutly to be hoped that the United States may have the honor (very easily obtained) of setting the first example, among the tributaries, of chastising the indolence of their horde."

William Eaton

Four years before O'Bannon was appointed Second Lieutenant in the U. S. M. C., William Eaton was appointed by Secretary of State Timothy Pickering in 1797 to be the U. S. Consul at Tunis. The choice of a maverick such as Eaton, an undisciplined soldier of fortune, as the U. S. representative in the explosive Barbary powder keg appeared to be reckless and ridiculous. On the other hand, Pickering was shrewd enough to see in Eaton a stubborn Yankee, who shared the opinion of the Secretary of State that the United States could no longer tolerate the scandalous acts of piracy. Perhaps Pickering reasoned that if such great men as Franklin, Adams and Jefferson had failed in this impossible mission, a completely new approach was needed in diplomacy. Whether he bargained for something sensational is something else.

While O'Bannon was participating in rather routine maneuvers off the Barbary Coast, watching Commodore Richard Dale try a Tripolitan blockade and then sail home, only to be replaced by Commodore Richard Morris, who was equally ineffective, Eaton set about on his mission to get the Bey of Tunis to modify his exorbitant demands. It was hoped that this would then have a beneficial effect on Yusef of Tripoli. Eaton had been ordered to stop at an Algierian chieftain's throne to pay his respects. However, Eaton was so repulsed by the degradation he was subjected to in the form of insults, kissing the Bey's fat hand, and the self-emolation expected of him that he exclaimed, "Can any man believe that this elevated brute has seven kings of Europe, two republics and a continent, tributary to him, when his whole naval force is not equal to two lines of battle ships? It is so."

Desperate, Eaton returned home in order to explain to Congress the plan he and James L. Cathcart, Consular Agent to Tripoli, proposed to "divide and conquer the enemy" on land by returning the ex-Pasha Hamet Karamanli to power in Derna. This would require deposing Yusef Karamanli, Hamet's brother, who had previously seized the power and the glory from Hamet, and recognizing Hamet as the legitimate ruler of Tripoli. They had great confidence that Hamet would agree to freedom of the seas and international laws. After considerable delay, President Jefferson supported the Eaton-Cathcart plan and had Eaton appointed a special "naval agent to the several Barbary regencies." William Eaton also presented a claim to Congress of $22,000 of personal funds he had already advanced to Bashaw Hamet. Meanwhile the Navy was stepping up its own activities under the dynamic leadership of Commander Edward Preble, but Preble was outranked by Commodore Samuel Barron, who was extremely cool toward "Mister" Eaton, as he bluntly addressed him, and was not the least bit enthusiastic about his conspiratory plan to support Hamet and overthrow Hamet's brother Yusef, the reigning Bashaw of Tripoli.

In November, 1804, Barron wrote the following secret orders to Lt. Isaac Hull, captain of the sloop-of-war, U.S.S. Argus:

> The written orders I here hand you, to proceed to the port of Alexandria or Smyrna, for convoying to Malta any vessel you may find there, are intended to disguise the real object of your expedition, which is to proceed with Mr. Eaton to Alexandria, in search of Hamet Bashaw, the rival brother and legitimate sovereign of the reigning Bashaw of Tripoli; and to convey him and his suite to Derna, or such other place on the coast as may be determined the most proper for co-operating with the naval force under my command, against the common enemy.

At last William Eaton was ready to begin his great adventure with Lt. O'Bannon as his right hand man. Eaton's "personal gear boxes" secretly contained U.S. rifles, his tent, scimitar and assorted field equipment. After the arms arrived in Cairo, Lt. O'Bannon, who had been commanding the Marines of the Argus was chosen to command a small party of Marines to act as Naval Agent Eaton's "bodyguards," more diplomatically referred to as "escorts." Eaton's orders were clear and concise, at least that is what the U.S. Navy commanders on the Barbary Coast thought. Eaton would find Hamet Karamanli, give him arms and money and help him organize an army that would invade Tripoli in April or May by land while Commander-in-Chief of the Mediterranean squadron Commander John Rodgers attacked from the sea. However, by February, 1805, Lt. O'Bannon, his midshipman and his six enlisted men had a somewhat more exciting vision of Eaton's aspirations and plans to lead his own army in Hamet's name across the Libyan Desert, attack Derna, return Hamet to power in Tripoli (thus restoring a ruler who would be a friend of the U.S.) and put a stop to the greedy demands and inhuman acts of Yusef. O'Bannon knew the scope and nature of Eaton's plan but said nothing to Lt. Hull about this unorthodox Naval Agent. Apparently he and the other marines were as eager for adventure as Eaton and regarded the prospect of a journey across hundreds of miles of treacherous desert as a fascinating, if not patriotic, challenge.

In spite of the fact that Eaton was getting the "go" signal from some quarters, distrust, suspicion and doubt filtered in from other sources that would have discouraged a man of less confidence and determination. Commodore Barron insisted it would not be discreet or wise to send a full company of uniformed marines to take part in a Tripolitan coup d'etat, so Eaton forged ahead with his own bizarre plans while British authorities helped him buy supplies and recruit more volunteers in Alexandria. During the preparations for the march and attack on Yusuf, Lt. Isaac Hull became increasingly apprehensive that Eaton planned to become the commander-in-chief of his strange army and might cause embarrassment for the Navy and serious trouble for a fledgling nation. Hull was also suspicious about the types of recruits that Eaton was attracting to his campaign. Rumors were circulating that most of Eaton's mercenaries were ex-convicts, cutthroats, impostors and unscrupulous Arab blackmailers.

Furthermore, the curious and eccentric things about Eaton's attire, speech and behavior that O'Bannon found intriguing, Hull regarded as obnoxious. For example, early in the year 1805 Eaton, now deeply tanned, discarded western attire for flowing Arab robes, a pair of pistols and a dazzling scimitar in his belt. He spoke four Arab dialects fluently as well as four or five other languages and several North American Indian dialects, handled the scimitar like a formidable swordsman and rode a spirited stallion superbly. Much to the chagrin of Lt. O'Bannon, who was responsible for Eaton's safety, he had limitless energy and was utterly fearless in any situation. During this time of search for Hamet, O'Bannon and Eaton "passed as American officers of the Army and Navy whom curiosity had brought from Malta to Egypt." Another source of irritation to the navy was Eaton's acquisition of the title "general." Now his comrades-in-arms were addressing him in this manner and the Naval Agent was referring to himself and signing his letters and papers, "General William Eaton." General Eaton was in his glory.

Although O'Bannon and Eaton were destined for adventure, they were not destined for an easy road to glory. The Lieutenant and the General and their "irregulars" ran head-on into one obstacle after another before they ever started the march to Derna. Eaton's funds were quickly slipping through his fingers, Hull could not promise additional money to finance the expeditions and in spite of searches, bribes, promises and guarantees of personal safety, Hamet could not be persuaded to come out of hiding. In January 1805, Eaton received a message from Hamet suggesting that they meet in a small oasis near Minyeh. Against the pleas of everyone from the Turkish viceroy to his hired soldiers, Eaton set out across the Egyptian desert with his entire entourage to Minyeh, which was about 200 miles south of Alexandria. At Damanhur they were captured by Turks and held in separate cells for treason. Luckily, within a short period of time, Eaton had charmed the rusks into providing him with a suite of rooms, releasing his men from jail and agreeing to let him meet Hamet in Damanhur.

In mid-January the elusive Hamet arrived at Damanhur and General Eaton, using every argument he could think of, convinced Hamet that he should join them immediately to regain his heritage and act as their "official" leader. No sooner had Hamlet agreed to go along with the military plan of returning as Derna's ruler than Eaton was informed that a false rumor reached Alexandria to the effect that the American flag had been raised at Damanhur. The Governor was demanding an apology and would refuse to allow Hamet and his group to enter the city gates. Afraid that Hamet would change his mind about the venture to Derna, Eaton and his motley group headed for Burj el Arab, forty miles west of Alexandria to wait there for additional Tripolitan recruits. Without Hamet and without Tripolitan fighters, the invasion would not appear legal or moral in the eyes of the world and the conduct of the United States might even be more questionable and unsavory than Yusuf's in demanding tributes from his victims.

In spite of infinite complications and impossible odds, General Eaton's final plans for the Libyan desert march began to shape up quite well. Still worried that Eaton might lead the troops himself, Hull and Barron comforted themselves by believing that no American in his right mind would consider trudging across hundreds of miles of desert leading a group of unruly, untrustworthy opportunists. They were confident that the Navy could easily take Derna without any land supports and that Eaton would return to the squadron now that he had found Hamet Karamanli.

They were wrong.

CHAPTER THREE

O'BANNON FINDS A HERO

"Tell Mr. O'Bannon all his shipmates are well and very anxious to hear his description of the Nile."

Letter from Hull to Eaton

Just when it looked as if things were going well for General Eaton and Lt. O'Bannon, the Governor of Alexandria sent troops to confiscate Eaton's goods and supplies. Lt. O'Bannon, who was standing guard duty with his small group of marines, directly ordered the Turkish officer to leave. Soon the officer returned with the augmented support of a Turkish battalion, but O'Bannon would not budge, compromise or give in. Shortly after this second encounter, an entire Turkish infantry regiment demanded the equipments but O'Bannon was not one to be intimidated. One U.S. Marine Corps officer and seven enlisted men were holding at bay an entire hostile regiment in a manner that was to become part of Marine Corps pride and tradition.

Staunchly supporting O'Bannon's adamant stand, an irate General Eaton stormed the Alexandrian Governor, swore, indulged in saber rattling and threats which proved effective and resulted in the General's permission to keep his supplies and spend more time recruiting officers in Alexandria.

Eli Danielson, Eaton's stepson, who served as his personal aide-de-camp, shared O'Bannon's growing conviction that General Eaton was one of the greatest men who had ever lived. Although it was his flair for the dramatic that initially caught ones attention, Eaton was admired by his men because he really was their superior in everything he did. He could ride as well as the best Bedouin horseman, could match any marksman with the rifle, and could handle a cannon expertly. He had enormous resources of energy, never complained of thirst, fatigue or hunger and knew how to brandish a terrible, swift scimitar. "The General," wrote Lt. O'Bannon, "always knows what to say and do, in any situation." O'Bannon then went on to tell the tale about the day 450 Arabs in their army mutinied. The General handed a stunned O'Bannon his rifle, pistols and scimitar and went into their midst unarmed. O'Bannon was beside himself and considered giving orders to his men to disperse the swarming throng with fixed bayonets, but he was afraid the mutineers would kill Eaton before he could reach his side. The young Lieutenant was frantic, blaming himself for negligence and incompetence. Much to his amazement, O'Bannon could hear Eaton's voice over the mob of hysterical, shouting Arabs. Eaton was ridiculing and insulting them, calling them women who were afraid of battle and cowards who would run away rather than "taste the glory that would belong to those who captured Derna from the Bey Yusuf."

O'Bannon was further shocked that Bey Hamet Karamanli was himself participating in the mutiny, but soon observed that as Eaton continued his oratory, Hamet hid his face in his hands and began to weep pitifully. Other Arabs began to weep, cover their faces and beg forgiveness for their cowardice. At that point in the confrontation, O'Bannon noticed that the General's manner changed from castigation to one of encouragement and joy. Soon the Arabs were cheering him, lifting him onto their shoulders and marching him around the camp, singing, laughing and crying.

"When the General decided there had been enough of the parade," recorded O'Bannon, "he commanded them to put him down and go about their business. They obeyed him with alacrity and the mutiny came to a swift and inglorious end. But the General was not yet finished with the insurrectionists. He had singled out two fellows who were the ringleaders of the uprising, and after he had recovered his weapons from me, sent for them."

When the men approached him, General Eaton explained to them that they were guilty of breaking the basic military law, that of loyalty and obedience to their commanding officer and that they would have to pay the penalty for their transgression. "So saying," wrote O'Bannon, "he drew his scimitar and decapitated each of them with a single stroke, performing this grisly act with a tranquility of spirit astonishing in one who so frequently displayed a tenderness to all of his fellow human beings.

"Therefore, he had the dripping heads of the culprits mounted on pikes and placed in the rock wasteland beyond the oasis. There, when the march resumed, the other Arabs saw what had happened to their comrades, and learned a salutary lesson." The anti-climax to the whole frenetic adventure occurred that evening after dinner. Lt. O'Bannon was respectfully but fervently taking the General to task for his reckless abandon in confronting the treacherous Arabs while he was totally unarmed. In his records O'Bannon reported the sequel this way: "By way of reply, the General laughed and raised the sleeves of his loose-fitting Arabian robe. There I could see, lightly strapped to his wrists and lower arms, two superbly fine-balanced knives with bone handles, which he can throw great distances, and with remarkable accuracy. A slight tug at the handle of either knife would have brought the weapon instantly into his hand. So it was that General Eaton made a show of disarming himself before treating with the mutineers, when all the while he was prepared to take any violent measures required for his self-protection, had it been necessary for him to strike up a defense.

"Other men are tacticians who think only in terms of the one or two steps they intend to take beyond their own immediate, present actions. But the General is ever a strategist, one whose thinking is attuned to the making of plans well in advance, for any eventuality. Such a man as this cannot help but capture any goal he has determined to conquer. Those who command the enemy at Derna would be wise to lay down their arms when they first see the approach of General Eaton toward their gates! They may know it not, but they are doomed!" Such was the devotion, admiration and the confidence of Lt. Presley O'Bannon in the leadership and infallibility of General William Eaton.

CHAPTER FOUR

STRANGE SOLDIERS, SNIPERS AND SUFFERING

March 8 1805

"My followers would have fled to the desert, if it had not been for the firm and decided conduct of Mr. O'Bannon."

General William Eaton

"Mr. O'Bannon will enterprize with me the tour of the desert," laconically wrote General Eaton to Isaac Hull. Eaton added, "We shall encounter three dangers: a danger of robbery; danger of assassination by the wild Arabs; and a danger of being executed as spies by the Mameluke Beys." With that in mind, Eaton, O'Bannon and their Falstaffian army embarked on their Derna campaign. Although records differ as to the exact number of men and equipment Eaton had on his march to Derna, the following statistics are reasonably accurate: eleven different nationalities were represented including 500-700 Tripolitanian Arabs; 50-100 Egyptians; nine Americans (including Lt. O'Bannon and Mr. Peck, a non-commissioned officer and six private marines); 50 Greeks commanded by Captain Lucu Ulovix and Lt. Constantine; 80 assorted horsemen; a company of 28 cannoniers, commanded by Selim Comb and Lts. Conant and Rocco; a small group of Englishmen and Frenchmen who served as junior officers in the corps; Hamet's suite of about 90 men; 70 Christians who were recruited in Alexandria; a group of 300 Arab cavalry under the command of Sheiks el Tahib and Mahamat, including footmen and camel drivers; and 107 camels and asses. Later at Oak Kerar ke Barre they recruited 80 mounted fighters, 47 Arab families and 150 foot soldiers.

With the exception of the mercenaries, who were simply interested in making money and getting some of the loot, the men who joined up with Eaton and O'Bannon were all rugged individualists, who actually had nothing in common — not language, religion, heritage or education — except their love of adventure. One of the most incredible characters was a soldier who could have been called the chief-of-staff (if there had been a staff), a man who called himself Eugene Leitensdorfer, born in Tyrol in 1772. Leitensdorfer had fought Turks and the French and had enlisted in Napoleon's army. His experience included studying for the priesthood, being charged with spying, poisoning prison guards with opium, deserting from two armies, marrying a Coptic girl, and managing a British theater in Alexandria.

Some confusion exists about two men by the name of Farquhar, one Richard, the other called Percival or George. Richard, the elder, was dismissed on a charge of embezzlement, while the younger Farquhar was so resolute and affable that Hamet referred to him as "Mr. Far, like my son." As a result of Percival Farquhar's valor, Eaton recommended that he be given a commission in the U.S. Marine Corps. Another devoted follower of Eaton was his step-son Eli Danielson, who had attended Dartrnouth and had dreamed of a military career. Eli served as the General's personal aide; his father had been Brigadier General Timothy Danielson, a Revolutionary War militia leader.

Adding more color and talent to the entourage was Dr. Francisco Mendrici, formerly chief physician of the Turkish viceroy in Cairo, who referred to General Eaton as "The inheritor of the mantle of Alexander the Great." Whereas Eaton had been expelled from Tunis for lack of congeniality in his association with the Bey, Dr. Mendrici sardonically remarked that he had been expelled from Tunis for being too friendly with the Bey's wife. Some reports state that Mendrici did not make the entire trip to Bomba. The strategy of the campaign was to march to the Gulf of Bomba, receive supplies and much needed money from Captain Hull on the Argus and then capture Derna and the province of Bengazi, which is 225 miles farther west. Commodore Barron was directed to cooperate with the plan "... as far as he might deem discreet." Meanwhile, Jefferson had promised small arms, field artillery and a $40,000 loan to Hamet. And promises were practically all Eaton had to work with in organizing his army and offering rewards if they were successful in their daring expedition.

No dignitaries or bands were on hand to bid farewell and good luck to the raggle-taggle group of rogues and mercenaries and idealists who began their journey on March 6, 1805 along the edge of the Libyan plateau a wild, desolate, desert region, which was to "try men's souls" for forty-five days and nights.

Since O'Bannon had clearly observed that nothing on the campaign was going smoothly, from the necessary authorization of the plan, to the quality of the soldiers participating, to the equipment, itinerary, or climatic conditions, he was not surprised that the well at their first night's campsite was dry; there was no water within a six-hour march. Exhausted from a 40-mile march in scorching sun, the men used every ounce of reserve energy to clear out the well, which yielded a rather putrid water, which Midshipman Peck described as "worse than bilge water." For the rest of the long, perilous journey, the men suffered from lack of sufficient water and lived on rationed water, a handful of rice and two biscuits a day. To the Arabs, however, money was more important than something to eat or drink, and they made life miserable for everyone with their mutinies, demands for more money, extortion and delays in the journey which jeopardized the lives of all involved.

Prospects of a successful expedition looked just as dismal to Lt. O'Bannon the second day as it had the first. What a far cry the desert was from the lush greenery in the Blue Ridge foothills of Virginia and his great-grandfather's ancestral home in Tipperary County, Ireland. The problem this time was not foul water but rebellious Arabs. Not trusting the Christians, the Mohammedans insisted on changing the original agreement, demanding payment for their use of their camels at the beginning rather than at the culmination of the adventure. Eaton would not stand for this breach of contract; furthermore, he was infuriated at the start when only 107 of the 190 camels he had hired at $11 a head showed up. Having decided that their demands were out of the question, the General called their bluff and announced that the entire campaign would be abandoned immediately. The Arabs did some quick thinking and changed their minds about demanding immediate payment; after all some money was better than none at all. To reassure them there would be payment for their services at Derna, Lt. O'Bannon and the marines took up a collection from their own pockets and jingled the coins ostentatiously at regular intervals.

While the General had his herculean tasks to manage, O'Bannon was also beset by problems. It was a cause of severe concern to Lt. O'Bannon that the General insisted on riding ahead of his vanguard without escort or camouflage, a perfect target for enemy snipers. Twice during the morning of March 12, someone shot at the General but missed their mark. O'Bannon believed that the man was probably one of Eaton's own Arabs, perhaps an agent of Bey Yusuf Karamanli. Being used as a target for someone's rifle practice did not ruffle Eaton's feathers, but it certainly made O'Bannon and his aides edgy.

In early March General Eaton was leading his army along the sandy route that Alexander the Great had taken over 2,000 years before the Barbary War. Eaton's army trudged over desert land that Field Marshal Montgomery would traverse when pursuing the Germans under the direction of the "Desert Fox," Field Marshal Irwin Rommel in 1943. Camping near many wells cut through solid rock, the men that night had sufficient water, but not enough food. Without O'Bannon's guard, supervision and rationing or provisions; it is possible that the army would have starved to death before reaching the gulf.

CHAPTER FIVE

THE BRUTAL JUSTICE OF THE DESERT

"Every obstacle known to the East beset the army. Camel drivers revolted, Arab chiefs repeatedly refused to proceed. The Sheiks quarreled among themlselves; the Mussulmans plundered the Christians."

McMasters

Every day Lieutenant O'Bannon guessed the mileage of that day's sandy journey; it averaged about 20 miles. The shortest possible route would have been 520 miles across the Desert of Barca, the actual march was approximately 650 to 700 miles of scorching wilderness and overall about 800 miles. Although O'Bannon's chief concern was the safety of their leader, he was equally apprehensive about the route they would take, finding water holes and an occasional oasis since no one seemed to have much knowledge of the country or the terrain. However, within a week's journey from Burj Eli Arab, Lt. O'Bannon and his comrades-at-arms began to suspect that the General had extrasensory perception or a sixth sense. He could instinctively find the grass and water necessary for survival on the desert march. As O'Bannon put it, "General Eaton's instincts were uncanny."

And so the march toward Derna continued with the army's espirit de corps improving a little, but Hamet's patience and morale deteriorating.

It was Dr. Mendrici's task to calm Hamet's nerves and to try to console him when he was petulant and complaining about the hardships of the undertaking. Since there was scarcely any rain from March to January, the hot sun burned their exposed skin, the dry air cracked their parched lips and the shortage of water caused much discomfort. The would-be liberators of Derna undulated over the sand, up and down hills, through valleys and across bone-dry river beds with Eaton trading knives, baubles, costume jewelry and pots and pans with small desert tribes for some of their water supply. Not once were the nomads molested or robbed by Eaton's troops, largely due to Lt. O'Bannon's competency and alertness.

If the famous adventures of "Lawrence of Arabia" seem dramatic, violent and cruel, they are, in some cases, mild in comparison to several grizzly episodes that occurred on the way to Derna. For example, all of the men in this Falstaffian army were exposed to constant peril from guerilla fighters. Eaton had advised his men to suffer the indignities and potential danger and ignore the whizzing bullets whenever possible. This, of course, did not go over well with his hot-headed Arabs. Eaton tried to reason with his men that they would lose precious time trying to catch their antagonists, but tempers flared and tension mounted.

Realizing that something had to be done to keep his men in line, he organized a company of crack riflemen, who were to break rank when attacked and pursue the trigger-happy Nomads.

When this failed and anger was being compounded by humiliation, Eaton confided to O'Bannon that he had no choice but to lead a counter-attack himself. Riding in the direction of the gun shots, Eaton galloped ahead of his "Janissary Company" taking the nomads utterly off guard, killing one man with his scimitar, seriously wounding another and shooting another with a pistol. A few minutes after his counter-attack company arrived, the ghastly bloodbath was over. Death count: eleven men and five adolescent boys. Regrettably, this incident of retaliatory punishment was duplicated in encounters with several other ill-fated groups where no mercy was shown, no prisoners taken, bodies were stripped of their clothes, possessions looted, horses stolen and the dead bodies left for the vultures. Word of the gruesome massacres spread rapidly through the nomadic camps and soon there were no more guerilla attacks on Eaton's army. Eaton called for a halt of the troops just before sundown near the ruins of an ancient Roman castle at Alem el-Halfa. Here Eaton's men divided into three groups: the Arabs on one side; the Greeks and other Christians on the opposite side, and Eaton, O'Bannon and his officers in the middle. While the General and his staff were eating their meal (at his insistence they sat cross-legged and ate Arabian style from a pan of lamb stew), several Greek mercenaries came to his tent with a messenger from Derna, a former junior officer of the Bey Yusuf, who now had severed his relations with the Bey. The courier said that the Governor of Derna, one of Yusuf's men, had been thrown into the dungeon after an uprising and that Derna was now waiting to welcome Hamet as their legitimate ruler and Eaton as their Deliverer. As Eaton and O'Bannon suspected, the report was false, but it triggered off considerable trouble in the camp. When the men in the Greek and Christian camp began to fire their rifles to celebrate the good news, which they were gullible enough to believe, the Arabs assumed the camp had been attacked by other Arabs and decided this was the opportunity they needed to steal firearms, horses, wool blankets and leather boots from the Christian camp.

Although Hamet ran into his tent and practically hid in his bed, General Eaton valiantly leaped on his horse and galloped bareback into the melee. Twirling his scimitar, O'Bannon could hear him shouting, "I will cut off the head of any man who dares to fire a shot!" He didn't bother to lecture the men that they were comrades working for the same cause. They were natural enemies and Eaton knew it. Once again Eaton commanded his men and they obeyed him.

From that night on, First Lieutenant P.N. O'Bannon and the seven U.S. Marines slept on their rifles, while one member of the small detachment stood guard duty every night to prevent fellow soldiers from stealing their meager supplies. What's more, they marched the entire journey in full uniforms without bathing or changing clothes. Experienced now in dealing with chicanery, Eaton insisted on writing a detailed, formal agreement with Hamet, a covenant that included fourteen articles providing for every contingency he could imagine. It contained a guarantee for "perpetual peace and free, reciprocal intercourse between the United States of America and the Pashalik of Tripoli," the restoration of Bey Hamet Karamanli Pasha, the immediate and unconditional release of all U.S. citizens being held captive as prisoners in the Pashalik of Tripoli and even such remarkable terms as, "The tributes paid in this year by Denmark, Sweden and Batavia to Tripoli shall be paid, in turn, to the United States of America to defray the expenses of restoring Bey Hamet as legitimate ruler of Tripoli."

Lt. P.N. O'Bannon, Midshipman Pascal Paoli Peck and Dr. Francisco Mendrici witnessed Eaton's and Hamet's signing of this impressive agreement.

CHAPTER SIX

INSURRECTION AND MUTINY

"Lieutenant O'Bannon and his seven marines ... had their hearts in the work assigned to them as sort of headquarters guard, and the main reliance to get Eaton's motley army over hundreds of miles of burning waste, jutting rock, and shifting sand."

Tucker

On March 14 Eaton was faced with another insurrection, again the Arab's demanding more money. This time, says one report, the General offered only his promise, which they accepted. But after marching 200 miles across desolate desert land and overcoming superhuman obstacles, it looked to O'Bannon as though the entire, grandiose expedition was destined to fizzle out at the ruins of an ancient castle, Massouah, where a few families lived with a tribal sheik. The problem again was money, or more accurately, Eaton's lack of money. The Arab argument this time was that the $11 paid only for the distance to Massouah, that they had had enough of the General's army and were returning to their families. Sheik el Tahib, a treacherous, explosive, incorrigible Arab, supported the protesters who refused to continue to the Gulf of Bomba.

General Eaton and O'Bannon tried to persuade the camel drivers to continue for two more days, at least until they could get another caravan to take their place. Eaton scraped up every cent he could find including the Marine fund previously collected by O'Bannon for such an emergency and gave $673.50 to Hamet to give to the chiefs. Eighty camel drivers grabbed the cash and hastily deserted, leaving Eaton without camels or money.

Eaton and O'Bannon's misery was made more acute by a report that a hostile army had been moving from Morocco to Mecca through Tripoli to defend Derna. When Hamet heard the news, he was ready to stop on the spot, but Eaton contended that if the story was true, it was even more imperative to capture Derna before Yusuf's troops arrived there.

This stalemate was another incident calling for astuteness and imagination and as O'Bannon had witnessed many times, Eaton never ran out of tricks. It occurred to the general that all he could do was to cut off their rations. Eaton laid it on the line. If Hamet and his men would not advance with him, he would barricade his marines and loyal comrades and provisions in the castle until he could get a detachment of marines to come from Bomba to rescue them. Meanwhile, Hamet and the Arab tribesmen could find their own way back to Egypt. Eaton's strategy won again. Fifty camels returned for the two additional days and they all headed out of Massouah an hour before noon, only to travel 13 miles that day.

While these traumatic events were taking place, Commodore Barron (whom Yusuf had rumored to be dead as well as his brother Hamet) was writing a letter to Eaton saying that Hull on the _Argus_ would go to Bomba with supplies and 7,000 Spanish dollars. Eaton was promised ships, food and money, but there was no mention of more Marines, which he and O'Bannon desperately needed.

At midday on March 22 Eaton and O'Bannon reached the community of Oak Herar ke Barre, spent five pleasant days with the Bedouins, and departed with additional recruits of 80 mounted warriors and 47 tents of Arab families including, about 150 fighting men. Eaton was successful in hiring 90 camels at eleven dollars a head, to add to his depleted caravan, by offering his personal "I.O.U." Trouble pursued the entire expedition with the persistence of the Greek furies. The querulous Sheik el Tahib instigated another mutiny. This time he left with the new camel drivers, reconsidered, returned, and obstructed the army so that it moved but five miles that day.

While Eaton was often preoccupied with the rebellious Sheik, Lt. O'Bannon always had his hands full trying to protect the General from being assassinated, commanding his men, guarding equipment and keeping body and soul together. Although usually calm and imperturbable, O'Bannon was outraged at Oak Herar when he overheard a conversation between Hamet and the Sheiks revealing that Hamet was receiving a percentage of funds Eaton was paying for the rental of his camels. Once again the General took command of the situation, cut the rental price considerably and subtracted the amount that Hamet was receiving. Hamet accepted the terms tacitly but the Sheik protested. Eaton had had enough of the Sheik's antics. He summoned O'Bannon and his marines, who stood stiffly at attention. And although they did not intimidate el Tahib, O'Bannon and Peck drew their swords to help the recalcitrant Sheik "get the message." He did.

As soon as one problem was eliminated, another was looming to take its place. Late in March when the troops were closer to Derna than to Alexandria, two spokesmen and their armed Arab fellow-soldiers, confronted General Eaton demanding more money than they had been promised. Unable to deter the men who would not listen to his warning, Eaton executed the insurrectionists by shooting one in the heart and the other in the forehead. O'Bannon realized it was a calculated risk, for dozens of horrified Arabs could easily have assassinated the general on the spot. Instead, they hastily fled from the terrible scene. In his memoirs Eaton explained that by executing the conspirators he quelled the mutiny, saved the lives of the rest of the soldiers and made possible the completion of the march on Derna.

To make matters worse, Hamet Karamanli was getting jittery. O'Bannon and Eaton could see that the nearer he got to Derna and to being reinstated as the rightful ruler, the more petrified he became. At one point Eaton advanced toward Bomba and Hamet headed in the opposite direction for Alexandria. Two hours later Hamet caught up with the determined group and expressed his appreciation for their tenacity and perseverance.

Meanwhile, President Thomas Jefferson, the American consuls and the other three Barbary States were eagerly awaiting the outcome of the war with Tripoli. If the United States' plan won, it might be difficult, if not impossible, for the Barbary States to continue to collect further tributes from the fledgling republic. The encounter at Derna would be one of great historical significance, yet Eaton's request for one or two hundred additional bayonets like those of Lt. O'Bannon and for more marines was again rejected.

CHAPTER SEVEN

PERPETUAL DANGERS

"Eaton and O'Bannon and a few other rugged characters had to impart ... this lesson about the tough side of war to undisciplined Arab bands devoted to no particular nation and interested in campaigning only for what little money and booty they could get out of it. Eaton and his lieutenant were to learn that in the desert the human being often is less stable than the sands."

Tucker

As recently as World War II, with motorized equipment and supply trains, crossing the Libyan Desert was regarded as a difficult, dangerous military task. But General Eaton, O'Bannon and their men had accomplished this feat with foot soldiers, camels, asses, horses and unreliable troops. By trudging through the desert in April and May the men were spared the intense heat of summer, but they were, nevertheless, exposed to other hazards such as the "winds of fifty days" that darkened the sky and caused caravans to lose their way. Death could also come from penetration of the swirling sand into the lungs.

When Hamet's conglomerate forces were within a fortnight's journey to Derna, William Eaton issued a verbose, bombastic proclamation to the "Inhabitants of Tripoli" referring to them as "brothers." He explained the idealistic mission of the United States, castigated Yusuf as a "traitor and usurper of the throne of Tripoli and a bloodthirsty scoundrel," and asked for the support of Hamet, who, he said, would insure peace and friendly relations.

Ready to push on the morning of March 30, the frustrated army was thwarted again. This time the in-fighting came when Sheik Mahomet learned that Sheik el Tailib had cheated him. Demands, accusations, mounting rage, desertions, dangerous threats and further delays all contributed to a maddening situation. Eaton's patience with el Tahib exploded; he ordered the Sheik to leave his tent and threatened to put him to instant death as the fomenter of the camp mutiny.

In an act of unusual courage and leadership, Hamet rounded up the deserting chiefs and returned to a bewildered army. An impressive reconciliation took place the night of April 2, 1805, with Lt. O'Bannon witnessing Hamet, Eaton and the chiefs pledging loyalty and unity to the cause. O'Bannon was amazed at the expanding size of the army and the number of enthusiastic volunteers they had acquired. The following morning seven hundred soldiers, who with their families made a group of about 1,200, set out to face the perils of the Barca Desert with some rice and biscuits and without a penny to their name. O'Bannon's admiration for William Eaton never faltered, nor did Eaton's confidence that he had the ability to succeed in his "impossible" mission.

The pitifully meager supply of food and water caused considerable pain and anguish to the caravans and troops as they marched from Oak Herar to their supply site at Bomba. By April 6 it was necessary to slaughter a camel for food, trade another for sheep and eat a wildcat.

When they reached Auk bet Salaum Mountain, O'Bannon estimated they were 150 miles from Derna and less than 100 from Bomba.

It was at this point, when Hamet halted his columns at a water hole on the Cyrenaican Desert, that the Arabs and Christians came within a fraction of massacring each other. The incident started almost imperceptibly with Hamet's men complaining about the hand-to-mouth rations and refusing to obey Eaton's commands to head for the Gulf. Suddenly the feeling of mounting fury was transmitted through the camp and O'Bannon, Farquhar and Selim the Janissary rushed to Eaton's side. It is difficult to discern whether the General ordered his elite soldiers and the Greek cavalry to man their battle stations or to perform their manual of arms for a show of strength, but it is clear that the General and his entire corps could have been annihilated then and there. The Arab cavalry charged the line-up with lightning speed and someone gave the command to fire. O'Bannon, Peck, Farquhar and their Christian followers stood their ground. Grasping the total horror of the situation, Eaton dashed between the battle lines and startled the Arabs by announcing his immediate resignation as commander-in-chief and declaring that he would join the American forces at Bomba and return to the United States. He told them in no uncertain terms that he was fed up and that the mission was finished. They could starve, shoot themselves, be captured by Yusuf and executed for treason for all he cared. Incredibly, within a matter of minutes, the emotional men were rallying around the reluctant general, urging him to resume the march and again pledging their cooperation. Once again Eaton, against all odds, won the gamble and avoided total disaster. Lt. O'Bannon, in his testimony before a committee of the House of Representatives after his return home, described his leader succinctly when he said, "General Eaton always was able to read the minds and enter the hearts of the Arabs he commanded. He knew them better than they knew themselves."

It must be remembered that the interminable mutinies, infinite hardships and perpetual dangers of the 700 mile desert march could have been avoided if Hamet had consented to travel from Alexandria to Bomba or to Derna by ship as Eaton had originally proposed. However, Hamet refused to go by sea, because he believed his people would accuse him of deserting them and would abandon him as their leader. Eaton had no choice; it was either cross the Libyan desert or lose the one man who had a chance of establishing peace without further bribery and ransom, and of guaranteeing friendly relations with the United States.

Although the excitable troops were temporarily unified, by April 15 the food shortage had become critical. Hamet, hungry, exhausted and apprehensive, became so weak he had to be tied to his saddle. Men of the Bedouin volunteers from Oak Kerar ke Barre were too weak to continue. Bedraggled and discouraged, the vanguard cavalry reached the Gulf of Bomba only to find no sign of a ship or a sail across the blue Mediterranean. After building several signal fires, the men slept fitfully that night, but the following morning dawn was greeted by jubilant shots as the sails of the Argus were sighted. Said Eaton, "Language is too poor to paint the joy and exultation which this messenger of life excited."

As the realization of their great, perilous adventure began to dawn on them and as food and supplies began to pour in from the U.S. brig Argus, the Arabs regarded Eaton as one favored by Allah. Lt. Hull's reaction to the tanned, sun-and-sand weathered Eaton in flowing robes was somewhat different from the Mohammedans. The full impact of Eaton's accomplishment plus his fantastic plan to liberate Derna hit Hull when he heard all his followers referring to the Naval Agent as "General". Hull tried to convince Eaton that he was playing a dangerous, foolhardy game and explained he had absolutely no authority to act as a "General" to a foreign legion while employed by the United States Governnent. But O'Bannon knew that the intrepid "General" had been through hell too many times to be intimidated by some verbal lashes from a Navy Lieutenant.

Heading for an adequate supply of fresh water, Eaton, O'Bannon and the army moved slowly the next twenty-two miles and reached their destination on April 19. There everyone rested for three days. Whereas Hull's chastisement had little effect on Eaton, he was somewhat shaken by the report that Commodore Barron would not support the important Hamet-Eaton agreement. Eaton was told that he had no right to give sanction, support or promises to the exiled Bashaw and that his actions could involve the American governrnent in international complications which they had not bargained for ... or words to that effect. While the Navy was practically nullifying all political alliances and conventions, O'Bannon was somewhat encouraged by word that the Commodore did promise to support the land operation. For the liberators of Derna there was no turning back.

A report Eaton received on April 22 did not allow him much time for reflection or indecision. According to the message, Yusuf had about 700 mounted warriors, 300 infantry troops and about 300 horsemen coming as reinforcements from Tripoli. Fearful that the news would alarm his high-strung Arabs, Eaton and O'Bannon resumed the march early April 23 and sent a message to Lt. Hull for the Navy to blockade Derna on the 25th and start bombarding the walls of the province when Eaton's men appeared outside the city gates.

Lieutenant Presley N. O'Bannon, concerned that he would be recalled to the Argus now that the joint operations were about to begin, wrote directly to Hull saying: "Sir, Unwilling to abandon Expedition, this far conducted, I have to request your permission to continue with Mr. Eaton during his stay on land, or, at least until we arrive at Derna." O'Bannon and his small band of brave Marines had been such unflagging support to Eaton, it is doubtful that the General would have attempted the attack without them. Two days later in the strange battle of Derna the fates of Tripoli and of the United States respectively would meet head on.

CHAPTER EIGHT

"MY HEAD OR YOURS"

"Lieutenant O'Bannon and myself united in a resolution to perish with Hamet before the walls of Tripoli or to triumph with him within those walls."

Eaton

Lt. O'Bannon began to reassess his opinion of Hamet Karamanli after his arduous ordeal in bringing back the irate sheiks. Furthermore, he learned that Yusuf, the youngest of three royal sons, had indeed murdered his oldest brother, heir to the throne, and forced Hamet to flee for his life to Alexandria, Egypt. What O'Bannon had not realized was that Yusuf kept Hamet's wives and children as hostages in the Tripoli castle and that much of Hamet's anxiety, indecisiveness and vacillation was due to his concern for their lives, as well as for the three hundred American sailors captured from the Philadelphia.

As the army trudged toward Bashaw Yusuf's fortified city, they crossed a rocky mountain, and by following the Zawai Martuba road soon found themselves in the midst of a verdant valley, full of beautiful red cedar trees, all so green and lovely that for awhile O'Bannon might have suspected that his sand scratched eyes were seeing a mirage. The army was halted in the refreshing valley and camped there on the night of April 24. O'Bannon noted they were five hours' march from their military objective, Derna.

Bad luck continued to plague the expedition. A messenger threw the camp into chaos with a report that the relief army from Tripoli, led by Hassen Bey, would reach Derna before Eaton, Hamet and O'Bannon. The sheiks were panic stricken and Hamet was depressed and fearful. All along they had been led to believe that they would be able to liberate Derna with little or no bloodshed. Now it didn't look that simple. Hamet and the Arab chiefs held secret meetings all night long. Remaining aloof, Eaton and O'Bannon assembled troops at 6:00 A.M. while el Tahib and Mohomet led another of their well-rehearsed retreats in the direction of Egypt leading their Arabian cavalry. By now the Bedouins had caught on to this pattern of demand - rebellion - desertion and return; instead of going through all the trouble of packing up, leaving the army and then retracing their steps, they chose to stay calmly in their tents until an agreement was reached by both sides.

Within a short period of time Eaton instilled renewed hope and enthusiasm in his troops. This time not with one of his flamboyant speeches, but with a pacifier that proved to be effective even in the barren desert - money. After Eaton and O'Bannon distributed some of the $2,000 they had received from Hull three days previously, the sheiks returned for their share and by 2:00 P.M. Eaton's men could look down from their vantage point on a hill 200 feet above the sea and view the white, gleaming walls of Derna, the key port. Their target, reached after 50 days of struggling across almost 600 miles of sand, looked beautiful to O'Bannon but also formidable when he noticed gunnery loopholes cut in its terrace walls and earthworks thrown up around them. The origin of the stones used in the walls and in their buildings is not known, but it has been established that Derna had been constructed by stones removed front ancient Greek and Roman ruins. Scanning the lush fruit trees, groves of date palms, cultivated land and gardens irrigated by a river called the Wadi Derna, O'Bannon could easily understand why the Bashaws regarded Derna as a precious gem.

Derna had a battery of eight 9-pounders, and a 10-inch howitzer was mounted on Governor Mustifa's palace terrace on the western side of the Wadi Derna. Some Yusuf sympathizers in town had made loopholes in their walls and terraces to be used as a line of defense. The high stone wall, built in a semicircle around the town, served to deter land invasions, while two rather insignificant forts were set facing the Mediterranean to protect against sea attacks.

When O'Bannon and Eaton were not sizing up the situation inside the walls of Derna, they were straining their eyes looking for some ships on the horizon. On the day of their arrival, April 25, the situation appeared hopeless; not a sail appeared. Signal fires were kept ablaze and smoke columns sent up to attract the expected ships. At 2:00 P.M. they caught sight of the Nautilus but minus the two field pieces Eaton had urgently requested. Next the Argus and Hornet appeared with the Argus carrying the vital field pieces. Hauling the guns up a twenty foot high, perpendicular cliff was no easy task.

The enemy, seeing the artillery, assumed battle stations outside the town, while Eaton ordered Lt. Samuel Evans, commanding officer of the Hornet, to come in as close to shore as he could in order to give fire coverage to the army when it advanced.

Without believing the enemy would seriously consider the offer, General Eaton nevertheless went through all the proper motions of offering the Mustifa an opportunity to surrender Derna without bloodshed.

O'Bannon read the following letter which was delivered under flag of truce to Governor Mustifa on the morning of April 26:

> To His Excellency, the Governor of Derna
>
> Sir, I want no territory. With me is advancing the legitimate Sovreign of your country. Give us a passage through your city, and for the supplies of which we shall have need you shall receive fair compensation.
>
> Let no differences of policy or religion induce us to shed the blood of harmless men who think little and know nothing. If you are a man of liberal mind you will not balance on the propositions I offer. Hamet Bashaw pledges himself to me that you shall be established in your government.

I shall see you tomorrow in a way of your choice.

> William Eaton,
> Commanding the Armies of
> the Bey Hamet Karamanli
> Pasha.

Before Derna
April 25th 1805.

Eaton wrote the letter in Arabic. Under the same white flag, the Mustifa sent his reply, a masterpiece of succinct defiance: "My head or yours."

Curiosity and impatience now had added to Eaton's eagerness to get on with the job at hand. Against O'Bannon's wishes, he, himself rode with the cavalry patrols on reconnaissance. He reassured O'Bannon that no one would recognize him in his Arabian robes and bronzed skin. Incredible as it may seem, a guard had been derelict in alerting his troops and as a result General Eaton galloped right through the gate on the eastern side of the wall, and for a few breathless moments was actually behind enemy lines. What's more, he, Leitsendorfer and two Greek mercenaries kidnapped two of Mustafi's men and made a mad dash back to camp with their prisoners of war. In spite of the fact that he returned from his brash adventure unharmed, Lt. O'Bannon again lectured his commanding officer for taking such a wild, rash risk.

CHAPTER NINE

COMBAT

"We rushed forward against a host of Savages, more than ten to our one."

Eaton

Just as O'Bannon had expected, his "General" was calm and methodical during the final stages of combat preparations. He called his officers together for a council of war, briefed them on his plan of operations, and enjoyed his goat stew dinner and a mug of ale Hull had sent from the Argus before retiring to his own tent. After a good night's sleep Eaton arose at 4:00 A.M., had leftover stew for breakfast and made the rounds of his troops offering encouragement to his Christians, Arabs and Bedouins.

Checking the position of the American warships, O'Bannon saw that the Hornet and Nautilus had dropped anchor close to the shore and that Hull had sailed the Argus into the inner harbor to bombard the palace and other buildings. At 5:20 A.M. the Governor's guns opened fire on the ships; the flagship Argus replied by firing on the shore batteries with two powerful 24-pound cannon. Soon Derna was being hit by 38 guns. Within an hour of this assault the waterfront fort was silenced and the enemy gunnery specialists rushed behind the walls to reinforce the Bey's defenses.

There was nothing complicated about Eaton's attack strategy; he divided his army into four groups. Lt. O'Bannon was in command of a striking force of six Americans, twenty-four cannoneers with their gun, thirty-six Greeks and a handful of Arabs. A column of predominantly Tripolitan Arabs was assigned to Hamet, but were actually led by Selim the Janissary, assisted by Farquhar. The Arab cavalry was sent to the southwest with three orders: to prevent the enemy garrison from escaping westward; to prevent Yusuf's reinforcements from reaching the city; and to serve as a swift, maneuverable unit, ready to strike wherever needed. Most of the troops remained under the personal direction of General Eaton, who commented to his step-son Eli, "I shall taste my fill of combat before the day ends."

The exchange of gunfire between the American warships and Derna's shore batteries was Eaton's cue for the land battle to begin. Advancing from the southeast as planned, O'Bannon's detachment proceeded resolutely toward the fortified, loop-holed houses and wall until they were halted within rifle range by heavy counter fire. By this time Hamet's men had succeeded in taking some ruins to the south and had given Selim instructions to hold this position.

The hour between 2 and 3:00 P.M. was critical in spite of the fact that enemy reinforcements had not yet arrived. O'Bannon's contingent was like a group of sitting ducks for well-aimed muskets. Furthermore, one of his cannon's blew up, the other was damaged in the explosion and O'Bannon was left without essential artillery. The silencing of the enemy's port battery was now balanced by their demolition of O'Bannon's field pieces. Eaton, realizing that a standstill or a retreat would spell certain defeat, quickly came to O'Bannon's assistance with a small band of his soldiers.

Analyzing his alternatives, Eaton considered augmenting Selim's group, ordering the Arab horsemen to attack the west wall or concentrating the fighting on the southeast with O'Bannon. He decided upon the latter, gave a pep talk to his troops and then, much against the arguments and persuasion of O'Bannon, personally led the attack. While the enemy was somewhat stumped by the boldness of his charge, Eaton galloped straight toward the enemy as fast as his stallion would go, whirling his deadly scimitar in the air. Perhaps this moment was the kismet he had been inadvertently trained, conditioned and, even born for. Miraculously he rode through a steady barrage of musket fire, ventilating his robes with five bullet holes but escaping injury. Caught up in the daring deed and thrilled by Eaton's bravery, the Arabs swiftly joined their leader. One account says that the impetus of their charge was so forceful that it carried them through the trees and buildings of Derna right down to the harbor.

Now Eaton ordered O'Bannon ahead to clear the way. Hull, who had been witnessing the scene through his glasses, made the following log entry:

> At 3:05 P.M. Marine Lieutenant O'Bannon, with one midshipman, one sergeant and six marines, led a huge mob of Arabs down to the harbor, sweeping aside, like chaff, the defending force, which evacuated the entire eastern portion of Derna and took refuge in the western part of the city, which was ringed by its own inner wall. O'Bannon, although powder-streaked, appeared to be in a festive mood, and when he saw me watching him, raised his sword to me. I immediately returned the gallant officers salute.

O'Bannon immediately seized Ras del Matariz, the harbor fort and captured the entire enemy defense group there. It was at this very spot that O'Bannon, assisted by midshipman Mann lowered the Tripolitan flag and proudly hoisted the Stars and Stripes over Derna, an incident of historic significance giving O'Bannon of Fauquier County, Virginia, the distinction of being the first man to raise the American flag in victory on foreign soil. This battle was the first and only land conquest ever made by Americans in the western World until 1918.

The event was dramatically immortalized in a long poem, "Derne," written by John Greenleaf Whittier forty-five years later:

> "T'is done, the horned crescent falls!
> The star-flag flouts the broken walls!
> Joy to the captive husband! Joy
> To thy sick heart, O brown-locked boy!"

When one of the marines found the harbor guns loaded and in working order, the General sent his artillerymen to O'Bannon with instructions to turn them around on the town to open fire to support Hamet's drive on the castle where the Governor was seeking protection, and to shell the western section of the city. While Hamet took the castle and the cavalry charged from the west, Derna's defenders were leaderless and surrounded. Many made a frantic dash to escape. Some escaped through the cavalry position to join up with Yusuf's troops under the command of Hassan Aga, but the majority of the inhabitants were captured within the walls of Derna. The Bey had evacuated the castle and taken refuge in the mosque.

By 4:15 Eaton and Selim's troops met at the castle and the entire town of Derna was in General Eaton's possession. Only after his men had been victorious did Eaton confess that he had been wounded in the left wrist by an enemy bullet, an injury that was never properly treated and bothered him the rest of his life. Although casualties among the General's followers were remarkably light, the marines, who had been in the front line of battle all day, suffered more proportionally than the other groups. The names of all the seven marines who accompanied Lt. O'Bannon on the Derna expedition are not known. When Lt. O'Bannon returned to the Argus and resumed command of the Marine contingency he prepared a muster roll of the marines on board, dated August 1, 1805. Three of the marines on the roster were promoted, presumably the non-commissioned officer with the shore party warranted promotion from corporal to sergeant. It was probably Lt. O'Bannon's judgement that two privates also deserved promotion. These three were:

Corp. Arthur Campbell, promoted to sergeant
Pvt. Bernard O'Brien, promoted to corporal
Pvt. James Owens, promoted to corporal

Three others are definitely identified as casualties at Derna. Their names:

Pvt. John Wilton, killed in action, April 27, 1805
Pvt. Edward Stewart, died of wounds, May 30, 1805
Pvt. David Thomas, wounded in action, April 27, 1805

The seventh marine is still unknown, probably one of those included on the muster of the Argus.

Counting the musket ball that went through Eaton's wrist, there were fifteen casualties; the Greek cavalry suffered serious casualties. No official records were kept on the defenders, regarding those killed, wounded, captured or lost.

While Eaton was busy trying to get Sheik Mansur to release the Bey Mustafi from the sanctuary of his home, Hamet's Tripolitan followers scattered around the countryside persuading people to return to Derna to live under the benign, peaceloving, legitimate ruler. The chief interest of the Arabs, now that they were victorious, was celebrating their conquest. Whereas they thought the fighting was finished, Eaton and O'Bannon knew that it was imperative to organise their men in preparation for Hassan Aga's counterattack. To help out, Lt. Hull sent some sailors from his warships. A new stone fort was erected, walls repaired and things were put in readiness for an attack at any time. In the midst of all this activity, Eaton took time to write a thorough report to Commodore Barron. In it he praised O'Bannon, Farquhar and the Greeks for their "courage and gallantry." He said:

> The detail I have given of Mr. O'Bannon's conduct needs no encomium and it is believed the disposition of our Government has always discover'd to encourage merit, will be extended to this intrepid, judicious and enterprising officer.

In it he again emphasized his belief that Hamet's reinstatement at Derna was vital to the establishing of friendly relations with the United States and the maintenance of a long and lasting peace.

Although the victory should have been the cause of great satisfaction, Eaton and O'Bannon's confidence, optimism and equanimity were threatened by their fears that the triumph was also the beginning of defeat. They became disillusioned about Hamet's inability to unite the Tripolitans and about his lack of support by the people living inside the walls of Derna. Furthermore, both Eaton and O'Bannon began to get the unmistakable message that Commodore Barron was still not interested in supporting his plan to bring peace and to end piracy.

Perhaps Eaton's biggest mistake was his underestimating, the cunning Yusuf Karamanli. Seeing the handwriting on the wall, Yusuf seized the initiative and organized his own peace plan. Ingeniously, he set out to divide-and-conquer his enemies, the Hamet-Eaton army and the United States of America, by cooperating with the Americans, but by totally ignoring his brother Hamet. Actually, Yusuf was working on the same principle Eaton had tried in dividing Tripoli by pitting Hamet against Yusuf. To make matters worse, hardly anyone attached to the U. S. Mediterranean fleet pretended to be in the least bit impressed with the capture of Derna with the exception of Lt. Hull, who participated in the attack and regarded the military feat as one of significance in achieving freedom of the seas.

O'Bannon had shared his General's hope that the Navy would finish what they had started with a powerful naval attack on Tripoli and that the Tripolitans in Cyrenaica (Barca) would rise up and demand the abdication of Yusuf. Since neither of these events occurred, the battle weary marine Lieutenant found himself part of an occupation army that he had not quite bargained for. What's more, he knew, as well as Eaton, that the Bey Mustafa, Governor of Derna, still loyal to Yusuf, was using every moment while in political asylum to plot against Hamet and recapture Derna. When Eaton learned that enemy reinforcements had encircled Derna through the Bey's plots, he attempted to seize him as prisoner, but the crafty Governor was quietly and swiftly smuggled out of Derna on May 11 by Yusuf's partisans. Around 9 A. M. on May 13, Eaton and O'Bannon again braced for battle. This time they were the defenders of Derna against a counterattack by Yusuf's men led by Hassan Aga. About 100 of Hamet's cavalry retreated within the walls as fire from the Argus and Nautilus tried to aid Eaton's forces. When it was learned that the purpose of the attack was to put Hamet in chains and send him to Tripoli, he was escorted to the Argus where he remained out of danger the rest of the day. Hassan's men soon galloped away to the hills and an inventory was taken of the day's casualties: a dozen of Eaton's men were wounded, none killed; twenty-eight of Hassan's men were killed, fifty-six wounded, eleven critically.

Two days later Eaton informed Commodore Barron that he and his men were short of money and he again asked for reinforcements. Meanwhile Lt. O'Bannon realized that Eaton's life was in as much danger as Hamet's. Attempts had been made to poison the General and a high price was put on Eaton's head; the exact figure varies between $6,000 and $25,000 if dead and as much as $35,000 alive. Knowing Eaton's fatalistic outlook and stoic confidence, O'Bannon was not surprised when the General refused to take extra precautions and continued to walk through the streets of Derna without fear or bodyguards. O'Bannon's last military engagement in May was defending a group of Arab families who had been attacked by fifty or so of Hassan's men. O'Bannon in a party of thirty-five soldiers including Mann, Farquhar and Constantine, drove the raiders away, killing three of their men in the conflict. By this time Yusuf's forces were showing definite signs of deterioration, however Eaton and O'Bannon could see that time was running out for them also.

CHAPTER TEN

BETRAYED

"I have found my kismet in Barbary, but I am not so certain I like it."

William Eaton, to U. S. Minister in
London, Rufus King.

As the days dwindled into weeks, O'Bannon shared Eaton's bitter disappointment that neither Consul General Tobias Lear nor Commodore Barron would send reinforcements. They were confident that with a hundred or more Marines they could advance to Tripoli and overthrow Yusuf. They knew President Jefferson had given Barron full authority over Eaton's expedition, but neither the President nor Congress had planned nor anticipated the exploitation of Eaton and Hamet.

Ironically, while Tobias Lear was negotiating a treaty with the crafty Yusuf without Eaton's or Hamet's knowledge, allegiance to Hamet as legitimate ruler was growing and the inhabitants of Derna began to look at the Americans as heroes. They were awed by Eaton's fearlessness, and admired O'Bannon's defense of their city against repeated raids from the enemy. One account stated that just by marching his Marines through the city, Lt. O'Bannon was able to instill confidence in the townspeople, who cheered him with "Live the Americans! Long live our friends and protectors!" O'Bannon's personal charm in addition to his military proficiency engendered a charismatic effect on young and old, Christian or Arab, friend or foe.

Suspicions of Lear's chicanery were confirmed when the <u>Constellation</u> brought a message to Eaton on June 4 saying that the war between the United States and Tripoli was ended and that Lear and Yusuf had signed a peace treaty. Barron, ill and distraught for extended periods of time and unable to get the American fleet at Syracuse in combat readiness, sent dispatches that shocked General Eaton and Lt. O'Bannon. He feebly commented that Hamet was not worthy of support, that Eaton's covenant with Hamet was nullified, that there were no funds to help Hamet, and that Yusuf had those qualities which he considered essential in the character of a commander and a prince. Furthermore, Barron announced that he was stopping all arms, funds and supplies to Hamet, who would henceforth have to rely on his own resources. To add insult to injury, Barron's orders were then delivered to Eaton telling him to withdraw his troops and abandon Derna "with all possible dispatch." General Eaton's next humiliation was having to explain all of this to the destitute, deserted Hamet. Not being in a position to bargain, Hamet, in utter dejection, asked permission to leave Derna with the Americans on the U.S. ships.

In the darkness of night, the Greeks and mercenaries, as well as Hamet and his followers, were evacuated on boats from the <u>Constellation</u>. Eaton, O'Bannon and the Marines were still on shore when the people of Derna and Hamet's Arabs sensing their abandonment, rushed the last boarding boat with curses, threats, screams and outrage as they saw the "treacherous, dishonest infidels" pull away from the wharf.

An ingenious plan, an incredibly dangerous desert march, a courageous assault and the hoisting of the American flag over Derna's ramparts — all of this was one day to be part of the opening stanza in the U.S. Marine Corps hymn, but were events unheralded and unappreciated in June cf 1805.

"There were tears in General Eaton's eyes," Lieutenant O'Bannon later told a Joint Committee of the Senate and House of Representatives, "when he stepped into the gig. But he did not look back at Derna." It was little consolation to Eaton and O'Bannon at the time that the treaty contained the most favorable arrangements ever won by a Western power in dealing with Barbary pirates: release of captives with payment of $60,000 ransom for Americans Yusuf had held captives since the Philadelphia was seized October 31, 1803; promises of friendship without further payment, and the possibility of future treaties with other North African rulers. In the thirty hours Eaton worked without sleep before departure, he was able to make arrangements that guaranteed Yusuf's offer of amnesty to the people of Derna who had been loyal to Hamet.

Writing 76 years later about the affair, a Virginia historian, J.S. Blackburn, summed up the treacherous dealings with Hamet in one sentence:

> Such behavior on the part of an individual would be characterized by the name of "baseness; " but governments measure their gratitude by the power of the ally.

After writing to Captain Rodgers that Hamet had fallen from "the most flattering prospects of a Kingdom to beggary," Eaton requested that he be sent back to the United States. Apparently failing in every way, Eaton and O'Bannon had no way of knowing that they had both contributed enormously to the growth, honor and glory of the United States Marine Corps in establishing the tradition of valor and bravery against all odds, nor that they would long be remembered by the citizens of Derna who sang, "Din din Mohammed U Ryas Melekan mahandi," meaning 'Mohammed for religion and the Americans for stubbornness."

Stinging with bitterness, humiliation and defeat, William Eaton sailed for the United States from Syracuse on August 6, 1805, on board the Constellation. His betrayal by Lear was even harder to swallow when Lear wrote to him saying: "I pray you will accept yourself and present to Mr. O'Bannon and our brave countrymen with you, my sincere congratulations, on an event which your and their heroic bravery has tended to render so honorable to our country." Eaton's only consolation was that the United States government would provide for the future of Hamet and his family, but the grim thought remained on his conscience that his countrymen had already either fled or perished.

Before bidding a sad farewell to Lt. O'Bannon, Hamet Karamanli presented his "brave American" friend with a jewelled sword designed with a Mameluke hilt, which Hamet himself had carried while serving with the Egyptian Mamelukes. After the Derna evacuation on June 12, O'Bannon returned to the <u>Argus</u> and sailed with her to the United States in the summer of 1806.

The more he thought about it, the more upset Eaton became about the payment of ransom for release of American prisoners. In his opinion, Lear had not solved anything and in reality was perpetuating a heinous situation. One of Eaton's chief missions all along had been to compel the Barbary rulers to respect the authority and rights of the United States and it gnawed at his conscience and self respect to think of Tobias Lear destroying his country's image and integrity by paying $60,000 blackmail to Yusuf. In a report to Robert Smith, Secretary of the Navy, Eaton wrote, "The United States must be respected by the pirate nations, and we will never achieve such respect by paying blackmail."

O'Bannon's disillusionment was expressed in Eaton's report to the Secretary: "What have we gained by the war? What benefit has accrued to the United States by the suffering of the <u>Philadelphia</u>'s officers and men, six of whom died in captivity? What benefit has accrued to the United States by the death of two members of the Marine Corps who accompanied the Bey Hamet on his march to Derna? These dead, and the noble Europeans and Africans who joined hands with us in a noble enterprise — and who lost their lives in that effort — cry out from their shallow graves for justice."

Monuments to the man whom Lt. O'Bannon regarded as an immortal hero, General William Eaton, are a dilapidated pile of stones in Derna called the "American Fort" and an obscure street in Boston named "Derne Street." However, O'Bannon's and Eaton's sacrifices and spirit are inherent in the previously mentioned poem by Whittier:

> God mend his heart who cannot feel
> The impulse of a holy zeal,
> And sees not, with his sordid eyes,
> The beauty of self-sacrifice!

CHAPTER ELEVEN

BACK TO VIRGINIA — FROM PIRATE WARS TO POLITICS

"... for the first time spread the American eagle in Africa on the ramparts of a
Tripolitan fort, and thereby contributed to relieve 300 American prisoners from
bondage in Tripoli ..."

Joint resolution of Congress to
Eaton, O'Bannon and others.

The young Marine from Virginia was twenty-seven years old when his star and William Eaton's star crossed on the Barbary Coast, Africa, and the parting of Lt. O'Bannon and the self-styled General was as inauspicious as their meeting. There are no records to show that the two desert soldiers corresponded or visited after their return to the United States in 1805.

It is difficult to know if O'Bannon realized the historic significance of his flag raising over Derna on April 27, 1805. The fifteen stars and fifteen stripe flag that fluttered over the walled city, the first American flag ever hoisted over foreign soil in victory, was preserved for a while, but like so much of O'Bannon's story and Eaton's glory, it somehow disappeared. The flag was last seen in Brimfield, Mass. in 1820.

The voyage home for Eaton was a sad one. The usually ebullient, gregarious "ex-General", was melancholy and withdrawn, spending most of his time in his cabin brooding. If O'Bannon shared some of this gloom, his spirits were, indeed, lifted when he arrived in Philadelphia to be greeted with a hero's welcome. Little children and young ladies, before the days of ticker-tape parades, threw flowers in his pathway. Tall, with a fair Irish complexion, brown hair and blue eyes, Lt. O'Bannon was a handsome, glamorous figure. Admirers presented him with a gold mounted saddle and a white satin embroidered cover for his horse. The saddle and the cover have been lost.

Members of the Virgina House of Delegates, impressed with his military services, passed a resolution on December 26, 1805, which authorized the making of a sword, designed after the jeweled sword with the Mameluke hilt which Hamet Karamanli had given to Lt. O'Bannon after the conquest and evacuation of Derna. Unfortunately, this African sword, along with the flag, saddle, and saddle cloth have disappeared. Six years later, the distance between Alexandria, Egypt, and the United States was telescoped when the American copy of the original sword was presented to Presley Neville O'Bannon in Alexandria, Virginia, in the fall of 1811. The hilt was decorated with the scene of Lt. O'Bannon raising the stars and stripes over Tripoli. Until 1942 all Marine Corps officers wore replicas of the 'Mameluke' sword, made with an ivory hilt and enhanced with an eagle's head at the top of the handle. The Virginia sword is in the Marine Corps Museum at the Navy Yard, Washington, D.C.

Whereas the Barbary Coast pirates usually returned to their respective homes with bounty of gold, jewels and valuable supplies, Lt. O'Bannon returned to his Virginia home with such modest "treasures" as two exotic shawls and other assorted souvenirs of his two adventurous years in Africa. On May 20, 1805 Lt. O'Bannon witnessed a receipt given to Lt. Isaac Hull by General Eaton in the amount of $1,974. This sum was raised from the sale of 'prize goods' from on board the brig Argus and delivered to Hamet to help defray some of his expenses. Among the items sold (glazed cotton cloth, rice, blue linen cloth, turbans, shoes and caps) were 19 cotton and silk shawls. When Lt. O'Bannon applied his signature he added "Fort Enterprize, Derne." According to one account, he arrived at his parent's home near the town of Salem (now Marshall) Virginia, riding on an Arabian horse, one of a pair he brought back. The homecoming must have been a great event in O'Bannon's father's home, a modest "Potomac Valley," or "cat-slide" style house.

* * * *

William O'Bannon, Presley's father, was the son of John and Sarah (Barbee) O'Bannon and the grandson of Bryan O'Bannon who immigrated to the Colony of Virginia from Ireland early in the 18th century. Bryan O'Bannon followed the western movement from Tidewater Virginia to the fast growing region which was to become Fauquier County, and received a grant of 635 acres on the "north side of the Pignut Ridge" on June 26, 1728. At his death John O'Bannon inherited a portion of this tract, to which he judiciously added acreage. When John died in 1774, William received a "Plantation and lands on the East side of Pignut Ridge .. whereon he formerly lived." This would indicate that William O'Bannon was living on the tract of land near the future site of Salem (now Marshall) that was part of the Elias Edmonds tract of 2,000 acres, patented by Capt. James Ball of Lancaster County, Va. in 1732. Four hundred acres of this tract was sold by Elias Edmonds to William O'Bannon in 1770, and the rest of the tract was sold to him in two separate purchases later. His estate was divided in 1813 between his widow, Ann, and their children: William, Presley Neville, Jesse, Alexander, Thomas, Joseph, Agnes, Polly, Sally, Nancy, Bryant, Joyce and John.

On December 12 1806, William O'Bannon, then 77 years of age, made his will. Following his death on October 19, 1807 this will was probated on October 27. Presley Neville was devised under this will "one of the best beds and furniture" and was charged by his father to "pay every possible attention to his mother and see her righted in every instance."

Ann Neville O'Bannon, Presley's mother, thought to have been a sister of Brig. General Presley Neville, died in the year 1822. Her Dower Tract was divided at this time among the heirs still living. Presley and several of his brothers and sisters were then living in either Kentucky or Ohio.

The home of William O'Bannon was located about one mile west of the town of Marshall, on Routes 17-55. Nothing now remains of the house except several heavy, decayed timbers and two lone chimneys. Nearby is the O'Bannon-Lawrence families' cemetery surrounded by a stone wall where the tombstone hand-hewn of fieldstone with the inscription "W O B/--d Oct 19/1807 AG 78", can still be seen. The "Mansion House" (as it was known) was inherited by Presley's sister, Nancy Lawrence, wife of Mason Lawrence, and until 1969 remained in possession of descendants of this family.

* * * * *

The parade, promise of a sword and some comments of recognition were all very nice, but Lt. O'Bannon probably had anticipated a promotion in rank for his documented gallantry and for his services to his country above and beyond the call of duty. Disappointed when he did not get the promotion or even a brevet, the 29-year-old Hero of Derna, whose military career had looked so promising, resigned from the Marine Corps in March 1807.

His resignation was accepted with a two-sentence letter with no mention of O'Bannon's bravery in combat, self-sacrifices, leadership, heroism or exemplary Marine Corps courage and conduct while serving in the Mediterranian and on the Barbary Coast. The letter accepting, Lieutenant Presley O'Bannon's resignation read:

> Headquarters of the Marine Corps,
> Washington, March 6, 1807
>
> Sir:
>
> Your resignation as a Lieutenant in the Corps of Marines is accepted. I must here be permitted to observe, that your retirement from our service, I hope, will answer your most sanguine expectations.
>
> Your obedient servant,
> /s/   Franklin Wharton
> Lt . Col . Comdt., M. C.
>
> Mr. P. N. O'Bannon

Shortly thereafter, O'Bannon joined the First Artillerists as Second Lieutenant and later became attached to the cavalry. In 1808 he was made a Captain of Dragoons, but the appointment was never officially confirmed and expired March 4, 1809.

* * * * *

Although being accepted in the Marines had been the cause of much elation for O'Bannon, the event proved to be a thorn in the side to at least one person, Mr. Joseph Blackwell, the High Sheriff of Fauquier County. It seems that the Sheriff had appointed O'Bannon (who would have been twenty-four years old at the time) to help collect taxes and was thoroughly vexed when his young assistant up-and-left without providing a replacement tax collector.

Legislative Petitions of Fauquier County, Va., which are kept in the Virginia State Library, show that on December 15 1801, a High Sheriff of the County of Fauquier named Joseph Blackwell submitted a petition to the legislature requesting further time until the first of June to collect and pay into the treasury the taxes he was to have collected. Written in abstruse rhetoric and sprinkled with legal jargon, the petition opens with a two hundred thirteen word sentence.

Sheriff Blackwell explains that for the years 1800 and 1801 he appointed Presley N. O'Banion (the name was sometimes spelled that way) as deputy, who promised to give the Sheriff "bond with approved security for the collection and payment of the public taxes agreeable to law." In his petition he explains that his Deputy, O'Banion, failed to collect the taxes from time to time "... alleging various excuses."

As a result a judgement was obtained against Sheriff Blackwell for "the balance of the taxes then due with interest and damages." The petition goes on to recite that "soon after the above transactions O'Bannon left the commonwealth without coming to any settlement with your petitioner ... having left his books and papers with a friend to be delivered to your Petitioner by which it appears he has collected very little if any part of the taxes."

* * * * *

Two years after his resignation, Presley O'Bannon married Matilda Heard, daughter of Major James and Betsy (Morgan) Heard, granddaughter of General Daniel Morgan, in Frederick County, Va., on January 24, 1809. The renowned Rev. Alexander Balmain officiated. General Daniel Morgan earned great recognition as a hero of the Revolutionary War, especially for his gallantry at the Battle of Cowpens, S.C. General Morgan died in Frederick county in 1802 and under the terms of his will he left his daughter Betsy "All my land in the State of Kentucky ... about ten thousand acres." A codicil changed this and provided for his daughter during her life, and at her death, the several large tracts so devised, to pass absolutely to his grandchildren, Matilda Heard and her brothers and sisters.

Shortly after their marriage, Presley and Matilda migrated to Kentucky where they settled on the inheritance from General Morgan. The O'Bannons had moved to Kentucky by February, 1810, when we find him, "a visiting brother late of Saint Andrews Lodge No. 3, New York," at a meeting of Russellville Lodge No. 17, F&AM. Seven months later, on 22 September, he was admitted a member of the Lodge. Presley Neville's holdings in Virginia were sold in 1818 to his brother, Thomas.

* * * * *

In the following years, while O'Bannon was settling down to civilian life, William Eaton, a homeless hero, continued to badger Congress to wipe out piracy, keep promises to Hamet Karamanli and to assert its influence abroad. He gave boisterous speeches about America's honor and almost became seriously entangled in Aaron Burr's treasonable plot to establish a separate American empire in the SouthWest. No longer seeking immortality or adventure, Eaton was committed to helping the United States recover "the honorable position she deserves in the Barbary States." Said Eaton, "I am prepared to fight for this cause until the end of my days."

Six years after his "one bright shining moment" shared with Lt. O'Bannon behind the gleaming white walls of Derna when they liberated the city, the "Barbary General" was dead.

After suffering a long period of illness and being handicapped by a crippling disease, William Eaton died at 9 A.M. June 1, 1811, a few months before the State of Virginia presented a sword of appreciation to Presley O'Bannon.

Decades after Eaton's death, Senator Thomas Hart Benton of Missouri introduced a bill of pension for the incorrigible Leitensdorfer, Eaton and O'Bannon's desert comrade-in-arms, and casually asked, "By the way, what did we ever do about old Eaton?" The answer, of course, was "nothing."

* * * * *

After moving to Kentucky Mr. O'Bannon launched his political career, and from the vast number of land transactions in Russellville, entered the real estate business too. He was appointed a representative from Logan County, Ky., to the State Legislature in 1812 and was re-elected to the House of Representatives for the next nine years. From 1824 to 1826 he served as Senator from Logan County.

Accounts differ regarding his children. Some say he had two children who died young, Elizabeth Ann and a son named for General Eaton. Others say he had only one son, Presley Neville Jr., born in 1810 and died at the age of five years. Another report says the child died at birth.

* * * * *

Sometime before the year 1816 the widow of General Daniel Morgan went to Russellville, to live with her granddaughter, Matilda O'Bannon. The National Intelligencer, a newspaper published in Washington, D. C., carried the following notice of her death:

> Mrs. Abigail Morgan died May 20, 1816, at Capt. P. N. O'Bannon's, Russellville,
> Kent., aged 73. She was the widow of the celebrated General Morgan, whose
> patriotism and gallantry has justly ranked him with the Heroes of '76."

Of the 10,000 acres devised to Matilda (Heard) O'Bannon and her brothers and sisters by their grandfather, General Daniel Morgan, it is not known the numbers of acres she acquired. Sometime before 1832 she and Presley were divorced, presumably due to either problems arising from her estate or her mental illness was beginning to take its toll. On 23 May 1832 she and Presley were remarried, after agreeing to and signing a marriage contract whereby he "secured" to her "all and every parcel of property, real, personal and mixed now owned by her or that she may inherit or that she may obtain in any way..."

By 1843 her property had dwindled to "a houselot at Russellville and five slaves". On April 24th a jury declared Matilda O'Bannon "to be a person of unsound mind" and her estate was appraised for her maintenance at the asylum in Lexington.

* * * * *

In spite of heartache, disillusionment and disappointment, Presley Neville O'Bannon spent most of the remaining years of his life surrounded by devoted friends and lingering memories of his role in the Barbary War. He was described as a "man of rare sweetness and dignity and very popular." At the age of seventy-four, O'Bannon died on September 12, 1850, and was buried in a country graveyard near Pleasureville, Henry County, Kentucky, where he had gone to live with relatives. Seventy years later the Susannah Hart Shelby Chapter of the Daughters of the American Revolution got permission from the O'Bannon family to have his remains moved to the State Monument grounds at the State's Capitol in Frankfort. Mrs. Ella Pepper Dudley, a niece of O'Bannon, supervised the ceremonial transfer and reburial. A slab of Kentucky stone from Henry County has an American eagle and a cannon carved on it. The inscription reads: "Lieut. Presley N. O'Banion Departed this life Sept. 12, 1850 Aged 74 Years. 'The Hero of Derna' Tripoli Northern Africa April 27, 1805 As Captain of the United States Marines He was the First to Plant the American Flag on Foreign Soil."

* * * * *

And so the story of Presley Neville O'Bannon is remembered in a stone marker on his grave, in the opening lines of the Marine Hymn, in three destroyers named in his honor (in 1919, 1945, and 1979 respectively), and in history books that tell of his part in the Barbary Wars and his influence on U. S. foreign policy.

THE FURIOUS BATTLES AND LONG SERVICE
of the
DESTROYER O'BANNON

A tribute of significance to Lieutenant Presley Neville O'Bannon was the naming of three destroyers in his honor.

The first O'Bannon (DD-177) was built by Union Iron Works, San Francisco, California, on November 11, 1918; launched February 28, 1919; sponsored by Mrs. Henry O'Bannon Cooper, collateral descendant by marriage of Lt. O'Bannon; and commissioned on August 21, 1919, in San Francisco with Lt. Robert F. Gross in command.

For 18 years the destroyer conducted exercises and training maneuvers out of San Diego, along the coast of California and in Hawaiian waters. The O'Bannon, after creditable but uneventful service, was put in mothballs May 19, 1936 and was sold September 29, 1936.

The saga of the second namesake, by contrast, is a story of war, danger, and adventure. The second O'Bannon (DD-450) was laid down by Bath Iron Works Corporation, Bath, Maine, March 3, 1941. On February 19, 1942, the 2,050-ton Fletcher-class destroyer was christened by Mrs. E.F. Kennedy, great-great grandniece of Lt. O'Bannon. The ship mounted nine 5-inch guns, eight torpedoes, and 20 and 40-millimeter anti-aircraft guns. It cruised at 35 knots and carried more than 325 officers and men. Her first skipper, Commander Edwin R. Wilkinson, took command of the ship in Boston on June 26, 1942.

Most of the men on her maiden voyage had no previous sea duty. The U.S. Navy and Marines had stopped the Japanese at Midway, but had paid a heavy price for their victory, and it was anybody's guess where the enemy would strike next. The O'Bannon and her crew, like their namesake, lacking experience and specific military training, had to "learn by doing." Strangely enough, the history of the destroyer O'Bannon reads like the history of Lt. Presley N. O'Bannon's march across the Barca Desert and liberation of Derna in terms of "furious battles" and "against long odds."

After a shakedown cruise, the ship was ordered to the Solomon Islands area to engage in patrolling, convoying, and shelling shore operations. The American fleet at that time were occupied trying to intercept and destroy the Japanese fleet known as the "Tokyo express", which was making regular nightly runs through the center of the Islands in water known as "The Slot." These runs were reinforcing Japanese positions on Guadalcanal as well as attacking and tieing up U.S. naval units.

During the fall of 1942, the Japanese organized a large task force at Rabaul, New Britain, in order to expedite a major landing. Scout planes spotted the fleet and the O'Bannon was one of the U.S. task group which moved into the war episode known as the Battle of Guadalcanal. Action began on the night of November 12-13 off Lunga Point. The U.S. Navy headed right into the middle of the Japanese formation, taking it by surprise, and opened fire. The O'Bannon destroyed the searchlights of the 30,000-ton enemy battleship Hiei and was soon bombarding her with torpedoes. Planes finished off the Hiei the next day. The O'Bannon was also credited with hits on other Japanese units, which were also sunk.

The Battle of Guadalcanal inflicted heavy damage on the Japanese, but America suffered great losses. The light cruisers, Atlanta and Juneau were lost as well as the destroyers Barton, Laffey, Monssen and Cushing. The heavy cruiser San Francisco was severely damaged and an underwater explosion hit the O'Bannon.

After repairs, the O'Bannon took part in the shelling of the Japanese airfield on New Georgia island and an airbase being built at Vila where she shot down two planes. For three months the O'Bannon participated in surface strikes, causing enemy shipping losses and helping screen the heavy cruiser Chicago which was sunk off Rennell Island. On March 5 she returned to Vila-Stanmore for more shelling.

The story of the destroyer O'Bannon is synonymous with danger, luck, and courageous missions. In danger from intensive air attacks, she continued escorting a convoy from Guadalcanal on June 22. When the cargo ships Aludra and Deimos were hit, she luckily escaped and while still under fire she stood by to rescue survivors. She helped break up a formation of enemy planes off Lunga Point by destroying five aircraft without loss or injury to the crew or ship. She stood under fierce coastal fire on New Georgia to rescue survivors of a sinking destroyer Strong. On July 26 the O'Bannon was part of the maneuver which rescued 175 officers and men from the Japanese-held island, Vella Lavella. Because of the display of bravery and astuteness, the O'Bannon was given the nickname of "Little Helena" in recognition of her coming to the rescue of the disabled cruiser Helena and scattered survivors. Shells from the O'Bannon repeated an attack on "The Express."

This time with the support of the U.S. task force the enemy fleet was so badly hurt they could no longer use the Kula Gulf route for their supplies. O'Bannon's torpedoes substantially contributed to the sinking of the light cruiser Jentsu.

Just as Lt. Presley O'Bannon encountered one adventure and crisis after another in Libya and Tripoli, so the destroyer proudly bearing his name in World War II sailed from one dangerous situation to another. After running into the "Tokyo Express" in July, the O'Bannon, with three other destroyers, encountered four Japanese destroyers north of Vella Gulf escorting barges of troops to Vella LeVella where Americans had just landed. Attacking the enemy destroyers, the U.S. Navy was successful in defeating their troop movement in spite of heavy Nipponese air assaults during the operation.

The O'Bannon's next action took place with the destroyers Chevalier and Selfridge on the night of October 6 when they turned back ten Japanese destroyers trying to evacuate troops from Vella LaVella. O'Bannon torpedoes blew up the destroyer Yugumo and damaged two others. And once more the O'Bannon stood by for survivors, this time from the Chevalier, sinking from a torpedo hit.

The ship was awarded the Presidential Unit Citation for "outstanding performance in combat against enemy forces in the South Pacific from October 7, 1942, to October 7, 1943." Previously the Navy Cross had been awarded to the ship's commanding officer for the action of Guadalcanal, Jula Gulf and Vella LeVella.

After a much needed overhaul, the O'Bannon was back on the line at Aitape, New Guinea. On September 15, 1944 after months of convoy and patrol, she was part of the support for troop landings on Morotai Island. The following month she played an important role in the reoccupation of the Philippines. On one of those missions that sounds as incredible as some of Lt. O'Bannon's miraculous deeds at Derna, the ship fought off three separate formations of planes and shot down one while patrolling near the mouth of Leyte Gulf.

In February of 1945 she gave protection to landing forces on Luzon, which were part of the plan to retake Bataan, she shelled Corregidor to make way for·parachute troops, returned again to convoy duty to protect American supply lines and then hit coastal batteries near Ternati, Cavite. Floating mines and hidden Japanese gunners made this hazardous work. Serving as radar picketship, the O'Bannon also gave support to landing operations on Zamboanga Peninsula, and to the Cebu city area and Carabao Island. She participated with other fleet units and cruisers of the royal Australian Navy in preparations for the occupation of Tarakan Island.

During the last phases of the war, the O'Bannon was still in the thick of it, now supplying further carrier strikes against the Northern Honshu-Southern Hokkaido area of the Japanese islands. The parallel between namesake and ship continued to a climactic finale. Lt. O'Bannon participated in Derna's historic surrender to General Eaton in the African desert. One hundred and forty years later the battle-hardened destroyer O'Bannon was present in Tokyo Bay with the Third Fleet at the formal surrender and occupation of Japan.

Although decommissioned after overhaul May 21, 1946, the O'Bannon was converted to an escort destroyer by February 1950, redesignated as DDE-450 on March 26, 1949, and re-commissioned February 19, 1951 to serve out of Pearl Harbor. Her first tour of duty was with the United Nations forces re-pelling Communist oppression in Korea. She also served with the Taiwan Patrol along the coasts of Japan and Okinawa.

Between the Korean War and the Vietnam War, the O'Bannon conducted combined operations training with SEATO allies and the Seventh Fleet. Much of her 1966 tour was spent as plane guard for the Kitty Hawk (CVA-63), as the carrier's jets struck targets in South and North Vietnam. The O'Bannon fired shore bombardments on Vietcong camps, troop concentrations and small craft.

Rounding out a career of service as one of America's famous fighting ships, the O'Bannon went from combat station to recovery operations for the Apollo space craft and was also part of the recovery force for Gemini II space flight.

Still with plenty of steam, the O'Bannon returned to the war zone in 1967, operated as plane guard on Yankee Station with the Constellation (CVA-66), bombarded Da Nang, rescued the crew of an American plane which had been hit over the DMZ and escaped enemy battery shells during the operation.

The O'Bannon was still on the gun line supporting allies ground forces in 1967. The ship named for Lt. Presley Neville O'Bannon received the Presidential Unit Citation and 17 battle stars for World War II service and 3 battle stars for Korean War Service.

The third destroyer, USS O'Bannon (DD987), to be named for Fauquier native, Lt. Presley N. O'Bannon, was commissioned 15 December 1979 at the Ingalls Shipbuilding Division, Pascagoula, Mississippi. The O'Bannon was christened by Mrs. Robert H. Barrow, wife of General Barrow, Commandant of the Marine Corps. Among the guests at the ship's commissioning was Lt. Commander Kenneth O'Bannon, a graduate of the Naval Academy and a son of Paul O'Bannon, formerly of Marshall, VA and a collateral descendant of Lt. O'Bannon.

The present O'Bannon is a member of the Atlantic Fleet, homeported in Charleston, SC. She is one of the first major class of surface ships in the Navy to be powered by gas turbine engines, giving her a unique degree of maneuverability.

"A MAGNIFICENT ARM"

On May 2, 1941, Lt. Col. Charles H. Metcalf, Curator for the United States Marine Corps Musuem in Quantico, Virginia, eagerly opened a package containing a "magnificent arm," the sword given by the Commonwealth of Virginia to Lieutenant Presley N. O'Bannon in 1812. The historic sword had been in the possession of Mrs. Margaret Culver, great-great grandniece of Lt. Presley N. O'Bannon, who was proud to "loan in perpetuity the sword given to Lt. O'Bannon by the state of Virginia, for assault and conquest at Derna North Africa in 1805 to the United States Marine Corps."

Lt. Col. Metcalf, in accepting the sword on behalf of the Marine Corps, said: "The Marine Corps looks with great pride upon the brilliant career of Lieutenant O'Bannon and often refers to his exploits for material for morale building such as any military organization needs during these trying days. The exhibition of this sword to Marines will be an everlasting incentive to spur them on to make sacrifices for their country such as O'Bannon repeatedly performed."

The Major General Commandant Thomas Holcomb also wrote to Mrs. Culver expressing his appreciation for the sword, which he referred to as a "token of appreciation for the daring exploits of one of Virginia's sons during the war against Tripoli 1805." He went on to explain that the existence of the sword had been well known for a number of years, and stated that the Marine Corps had been very anxious to procure it as "one of its most valued trophies." The Commandant said, "Presley N. O'Bannon stands for the highest type of patriotic and hard-fighting officers of the Marine Corps and his career typifies most perfectly what is expected of a Marine in times of great national stress. I believe that the exhibition of this sword to Marines will always be an incentive to greater sacrifice and will be of material assistance in maintaining our "espirit de Corps"."

* * * * *

The history of O'Bannon's sword goes back to December 1805 when John Love, a delegate from Fauquier County suggested that Virginia honor "the gallant services of Lieutenant Presley N. O'Bannon, a citizen of Virginia, in the late war between the United States and Tripoli." Love proposed in a House resolution that the Governer and the Council "present to the said Lt. O'Bannon, a handsome sword with such appropriate devices thereon as they may think proper." Both houses passed the resolution unanimously and on January 7, 1806, Governor William H. Cabell referred the resolution to the Council of State.

It was then the responsibility of a committee of three councillors to select a suitable design. After more than six months of deliberation, the committee recommended that the plan submitted by Major John Clarke, superintendent of the Virginia Manufactory of Arms at Richmond, be accepted. Major Clarke's designs were both impressive and ostentatious. His sketches included the head of a turbanned and bearded Moslem warrior; a scene showing "the intrepid O'Bannon while in the act of rearing the American standard"; and a captured American at the entrance of a dungeon to illustrate that "the object of the enterprise in which this officer distinguished himself" was the liberation of prisoners. The guard of the sword was decorated with the Virginia coat-of-arms, the American eagle, and the heads of Ares, Greek God of War, and Poseidon, God of the ocean.

Clarke, however, was more interested in his intricate designs than he was in getting his facts straight. He got his information about the historic event from a newspaper article he "cursorily read" and as a result misspelled O'Bannon's Christian name as "Priestly" in the inscription that appears on the blade.

In addition to the sword, Clarke also had planned a silver scabbard and a belt "of buff leather, stitched with silver thread and adorned with a golden crescent." Still not elaborate enough for Clarke's taste, the crescent was to have the picture of three American warships bombarding the fortress of Derna engraved upon it.

Clarke started working on the sword during the summer of 1806 and told Delegate John Love that the weapon would soon be completed. Unfortunately, it was still not ready three years later when Clarke was relieved of his duties as superintendent of the Manufactory of Arms. In October of 1809 the new Governor, John Tyler, Sr., and the Council again brought up the subject of O'Bannon's promised sword. They preferred a simpler design for the weapon, and commissioned John M. Carter of Richmond to make the hilt, scabbard and belt, "the blade thereof being furnished by the Commonwealth." Carter agreed to finish engraving O'Bannon's "sword of honor" with all its accouterments for $240. From this amount Carter had to spend $80 for the gold and silver used in the hilt and its ornaments.

After encountering "many unforeseen difficulties" in the process of executing the sword, Carter finished the weapon, in the simplified version, in July 1810. In place of the silver scabbard Clarke had designed, there was a leather sheath "mounted with a silver tip." An eagle's head replaced the Turk's head on the pommel. Instead of being solid metal, the pommel was made of "a thin sheaf of silver filled with lead." A gold medallion appeared on the hilt showing O'Bannon raising the American flag, and all of the original trimmings were eliminated.

Ironically, all that remained of Clarke's effort was the misspelling of the hero's name. The inscription on the blade read "... presented by the State of Virginia to her gallant Son Priestly N. O'Bannon."

After two Governors, Cabell and Tyler respectively, had their say about O'Bannon's award, a third governor, George William Smith proudly praised the sword as an authentic product of Virginia. The State Manufactory of Arms had made the blade; the silver and gold in the hilt and scabbard were indigenous metals of the state; Carter, a native Virginian, made the engravings on the hilt and blade and Reuben Johnson and James Reat, silversmiths and jewelers of Richmond did the mounting. Governor Smith announced that all this was "calculated to enhance the value of this present in the estimation of a Citizen of Virginia."

In spite of Governor Smith's eloquence and enthusiasm, O'Bannon still was not in possession of this great and generous gift from Virginia. While all the sword polishing and politicing was going on, Lieutenant O'Bannon had resigned his commission in the Marine Corps in 1807 and had moved to Kentucky. In April 1811, five years after the sword had been approved by the legislature, O'Bannon wrote to Richmond asking when he might expect to have the long-anticipated sword.

In answering his letter, Governor Smith said that the sword was ready but that the government couldn't decide on the proper place for the award ceremony. To simplify matters, O'Bannon informed Governor Smith that he intended to visit Richmond in the fall. Said O'Bannon, "I will then have the pleasure of receiving from my native state a present of real value to me, as it will be a flattering proof of the approbation of my public conduct, which I consider as the most pleasing reward for my services." He also noted with great satisfaction that the sword and belt were made of Virginia materials and manufactured in the state. He said, "... it proves our independence of Europe, and also the progress of our infant manufactories."

For some reason O'Bannon did not travel to Richmond as he had planned and in the fall of 1812 he wrote again. This time to the fifth Governor involved in the complicated six-year project to commemorate O'Bannon's valiant feat in Derna. Perhaps realizing at this point that if he waited until the State planned a public presentation he might never get the promised gift, O'Bannon asked Governor James Barbour to have the sword delivered to him at Alexandria, Virginia.

Shortly thereafter, the sword was sent to Alexandria by stagecoach with a letter of congratulation from the Governor. The message to O'Bannon was: "What tribute of respect can be more grateful to a brave man than the unbiased resolve of the Representatives of a brave, generous and free people, announcing him to the world as one of its bravest Citizens, tendering him a sword as an emblem of his heroism, and, by committing them to record, consecrating, to after times his brilliant actions."

BIBLIOGRAPHY

Averill, Rebecca. "Brief Sketch of Services of Lieutenant P. N. O'Bannon, a Kentucky Soldier in the War with Tripoli." The Register of The Kentucky State Historical Society, Vol. 18, No. 52, January 1920.

This article is very unreliable, as evidenced by the title alone. Portrait of P. N. O'B. is one of his brother, John O'Bannon. For verification see: Ohio Archeological and Historical Publications, Columbus, 1905, Vol. XIV, p. 319.

Blackburn, J. S. and W. N. McDonald: New School History of the United States of America from the Earliest Discoveries to the Present Time. (Baltimore, Wm. J. C. Dulany & Co., 1881.)

Cain, John P. Lieutenant O'Bannon. Color-Bearer of Liberty. Unpublished manuscript in The Filson Club, Inc., Louisville, Kentucky.

Cooper, James Fenimore. History of the Navy of The United States of America. 2 vols. Philadelphia, 1839.

⸱ "Eaton's Barbary Expedition." in: Harper's New Monthly Magazine, Vol. XXI, pp. 496-511. 1860.

Edwards, Samuel. Barbary General. The Life of William H. Eaton. Prentice-Hall, c1968.

Fauquier County (Va.) Bicentennial Committee. Fauquier County. Virginia 1759-1959. Warrenton, 1959. pp. 177-181.

Lewis Charles Lee. Famous American Marines. Boston, L. C. Page & Co., c1950.

McClellan, Edwin N. History of the United States Marine Corps. Chapter XV, Vol. I, "The Tripolitan War" 1st ed., 1925. Mimeographed copy.

Metcalf, Clyde H. A History of the United States Marine Corps. Putnam's, 1939.

Montross, Lynn. The United States Marines: A Pictorial History. Rinehart, c1957.

(Prentiss, Charles). The Life of the Late Gen. William Eaton: ... Brookfield: Printed by E. Merriam & Co., 1813.

Rodd, Francis Rennell. General William Eaton. The Failure of an Idea. N. Y., Minton, Balch and Co., 1932.

Tucker, Glenn. Dawn Like Thunder: The Barbary Wars and the Birth of the U. S. Navy. Indianapolis, The Bobbs-Merrill Co., c1963.

The most complete modern account of the War with Tripoli. Contains an excellent account of Eaton's march across the Libyan Desert.

U. S. Navy Department. Office of Naval Records and Library. Naval Documents Related to the United States Wars with the Barbary Powers. 7 vols. Washington, G.P.O., 1944.

Wright, Louis B. and Julia H. MacLeod. The First Americans in North Africa. Princeton, N.J., 1945.

* * * * *

Fauquier County, Virginia. Deeds, wills, chancery suits, etc. (Clerk's Office, Warrenton, Va.)

Frederick County, Virginia. Deeds, wills, marriage records, etc. (Clerk's Office, Winchester, Va.)

ILLUSTRATIONS

Presley Neville O'Bannon, USMC
1776 - 1850

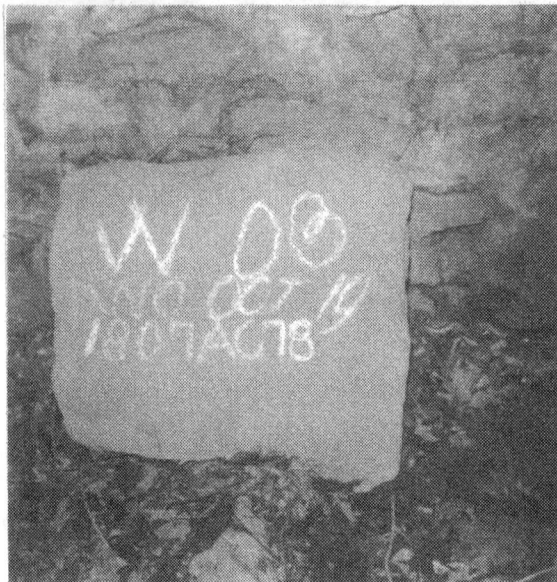

Tombstone at grave of William O'Bannon, near his home at Marshall, Fauquier County, Virginia.
It reads: W O B / Ano Oct 19 / 1807 AG 78

Birthplace of Lt. Presley N. O'Bannon, near Marshall, Virginia.
(Rear view, ca. 1930)

Front view of home of William and Nancy (Neville) O'Bannon,
parents of Presley Neville O'Bannon.
Lt. O'Bannon was born in this house in 1776.

Lt. O'Bannon's camel Marines on march
from Alexandria, Egypt, to Derna, Tripoli, 1805.
Courtesy U.S. Marine Corps Museum

This illustration depicts Lt. O'Bannon riding a camel,
before the final attack on and capture of the Tripolitan stronghold at Derna in April 1805.
Courtesy U.S. Marine Corps Museum

First Lieutenant Presley N. O'Bannon, USMC,
on the walls of the fortress at Derna, Tripoli, April 1805.
Courtesy U.S. Marine Corps Museum

Diorama: "The Capture of Derne, Tripoli, 27 April 1805"
After a march of approximately 600 miles across the Libyan Desert, a small force of American Marines, Greeks, and Arab tribesmen, under command of Agent William Easton and Lt. Presley N. O'Bannon, USMC, repeatedly attacked and finally captured a Barbary pirate harbor fort and turned its guns upon the enemy. The American flag, planted there by Lt. O'Bannon, flew for the first time over a fortress of the Old World, and demoralized the defenders of the town.
Courtesy U.S. Marine Corps Museum

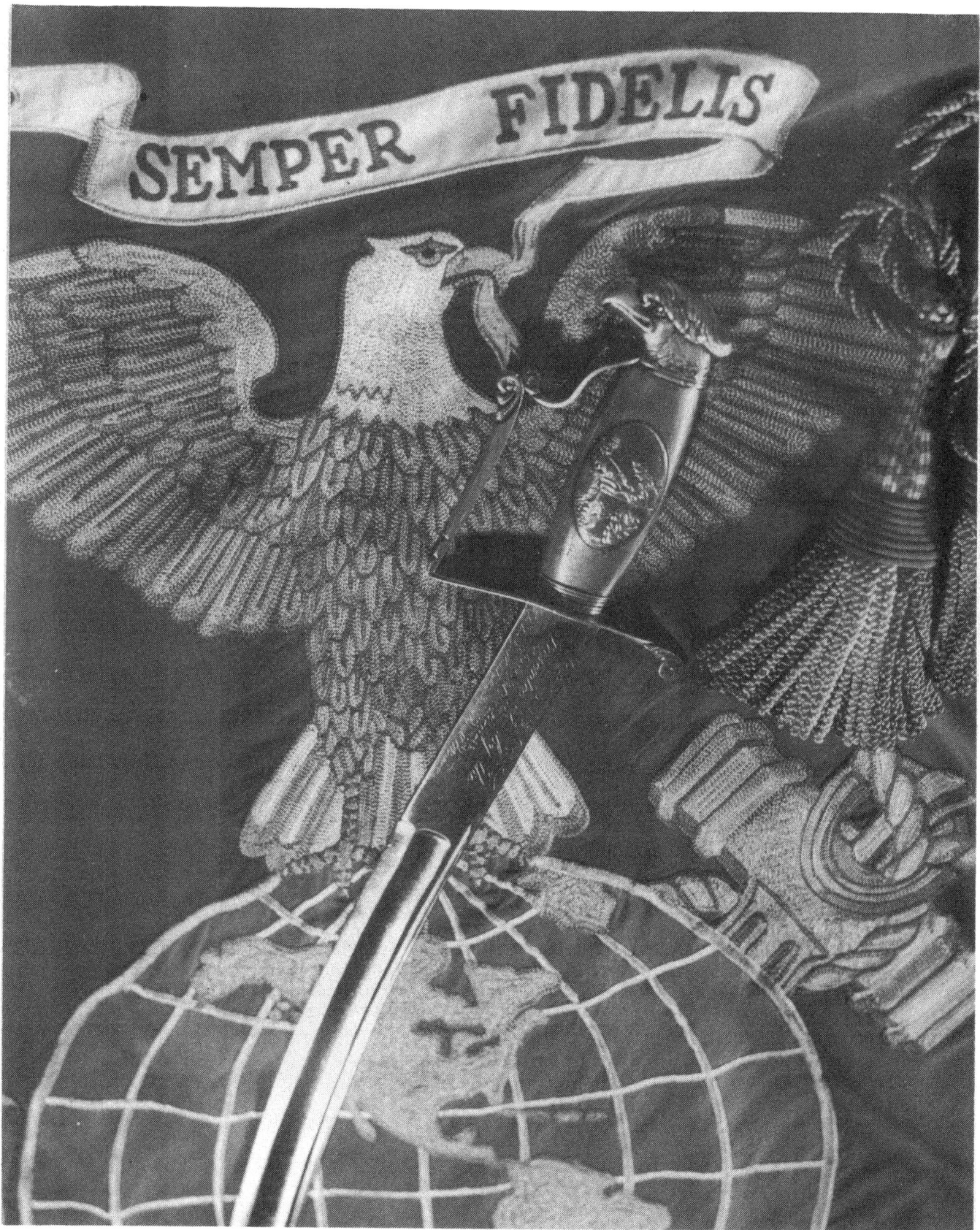

The General Assembly of Virginia passed an act on 26 December 1805 to award "the Hero of Tripoli" a "handsome sword with appropriate devices." The sword, after several delays, was presented to Lt. O'Bannon in 1812. Legend has it that the gold used in the decoration of the hilt was mined in Fauquier County.

The <u>USS</u> <u>O'Bannon</u> (DE450), the second vessel to be the namesake of Lt. P. N. O'Bannon.
The <u>O'Bannon</u> (DE450) was laid down by Bath Iron Works Corporation, Bath, Maine, 3 March 1942.
After meritorious service in the Pacific during World War II, the Korean and Vietnam Wars,
she was decommissioned 30 January 1970.
Official United States Navy Photograph

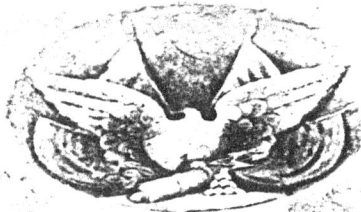

Lieut. PRESLEY N. OBANION

Departed this life
Sept. 12, 1850,
AGED
74 Years.
"THE HERO OF DERNE"
TRIPOLI NORTHERN AFRICA
APRIL 27, 1805
AS CAPTAIN OF THE
UNITED STATES MARINES
HE WAS THE FIRST TO PLANT
THE AMERICAN FLAG ON
FOREIGN SOIL.

THE O'BANNON FAMILY

Descendants

of

BRYAN O'BANNON

of

Ireland and Fauquier County, Virginia

Compiled by

John K. Gott

Dedicated to
the
Memory of

JOHN WILLIS O'BANNON
1847 - 1933

and his son

JAMES KEITH O'BANNON
1883 - 1965

and his son

JOHN NORRIS O'BANNON, SR.
1914 - 1986

Good Neighbors and Friends
Whose Memory Will Always Be
Cherished.

Table of Contents

USING THIS GENEALOGY

The system used in numbering this genealogy is the same system used in Dr. Horace E. Hayden, VIRGINIA GENEALOGIES (1891) and sometimes referred to as "NGS Quarterly System." The system, along with others, is fully explained in a National Genealogical Society publication, "Numbering Your Genealogy" by Joan Ferris Curran.

The system is quite simple: the first known ancestor is given the number 1. before the name, with a smaller superscript after the name indicating the generation. If the name of a child is carried forward into the next generation, a plus (+) sign is before the individual number.

Each generation is completed before a new generation begins. The ancestor representing the preceeding generation is given after the individual brought forward in parenthesis.

INTRODUCTION

This genealogy is the result of many years of research and study of the O'Bannon family — the descendants of Bryan O'Bannon, one of the earliest settlers of that part of Prince William County which became Fauquier County (1759) and later, commonly called "upper Fauquier."

The present compilation is not a complete lineage of Bryan's descendants. Not even a complete listing of a few who remained in Northern Virginia; those who we were not able to identify. To compile a complete genealogy of the descendants would take a lifetime! Many have spent that much time in accumulating and sorting data only to have it perish at their death. The case of the late Walter O'Bannon, of Tulsa, Oklahoma, is one example. He spent many years, with miles of travel and many dollars, gathering O'Bannon family records from all over the United States. After his death, in the 1960's, his widow refused to allow any use of his files. She maintained that their son "might someday" wish to assemble and publish his father's work. The years have passed and at the last report, both Mrs. O'Bannon and her son have passed away. We have no idea what disposition has been made of the files! There are several similar stories.

We do not know when Bryan O'Bannon arrived in America, presumably, the Colony of Virginia, nor do we know the name of his wife; whether she accompanied him to Virginia or if they married after his arrival. He was not the only one of that name in Virginia in the early 18th century. On 16 August 1715, one John Woodson was granted 1596 acres of "new land" in Henrico County, on the south side of the James River, for transporting 32 persons (Patent Book 10, p. 237). Among those for whom he had paid transportation, and received the land, was one John Bannion. This is interesting because of the spelling — very much like the early pronunciation of the name. And the same pronunciation and spelling used by many descendants today. The "O" is often left off the name, especially in Ireland, and by other branches of the family in the United States.

It has been the purpose of this work to compile the descendants of Bryan O'Bannon who "stayed at home;" those who remained in Northern Virginia, especially in the counties of Fauquier, Culpeper, Rappahannock and Stafford. Little effort has been made to follow the descendants who migrated to other areas and states. There are also several of the name in Fauquier County who have not been identified, *i.e.* Jackson O'Bannon who qualified as an attorney in the Fauquier County Court on 23 July 1838.

Several studies have been made, and published, of those O'Bannons who left Fauquier County for the South and West. Hopefully, more genealogical compilations will follow.

Many have helped to complete the present publication. Special thanks to the J. Maurice O'Bannon family of Rappahannock County, Pat Kerrick of Culpeper, Mrs. Betty O'B. Culp of Culpeper and Denton, Texas and her mother, Mrs. R.H.L. O'Bannon of Culpeper, Mrs. Katherine F. Weaver of Culpeper and Mrs. Martha (Barber) Armstrong of Williamsburg. My colleague of many library meetings in Fairfax, Linda Sudduth, identified all the Poes and Pearsons. Mrs. Nadine O'B. Olinger of Marshall helped with the Loudoun, Fairfax and Prince William O'Bannons. And, my neighbor, who is really responsible for my active interest in the O'Bannon family — Lou Bayly (Berry) O'Bannon — is due the thanks for whatever this study is worth. Words can never express the gratitude so many owe this thoughtful, generous and kind lady. Like the sands of the sea, her many kindnesses of generosity will never be counted, and typically, she wouldn't want even one grain recalled.

John K. Gott
Glencairn
Marshall, Virginia

THE NORTHERN NECK OF VIRGINIA

Fauquier County at one time formed part of a vast proprietary estate comprising all of that territory which afterwards became known as the Northern Neck of Virginia. This great tract of land "bounded within the heads of the rivers Rappahannock and Quiriough or Potomac River, the courses of the said rivers, as they are commonly called and known by the inhabitants, and descriptions of those parts, and Chesapeake Bay," was originally granted by Charles II in 1649 to Ralph Lord Hopton, Henry Lord Jermyn (afterwards the Earl of St. Albans), John Lord Culpeper, Sir John Berkeley (afterwards John Lord Berkeley of Stratton), Sir William Morton, Sir Dudley Wyatt and Thomas Culpeper, for an annual rent of six pounds, thirteen shillings and four pence, payable at Jamestown on the Feast Day of St. John the Baptist. This grant embraced not only the land "but the rivers themselves and all the islands within the banks of those rivers, and all woods, underwoods, timber and trees, ways, waters, and rivers, ponds, pools, watercourses, fishing, streams, havens, ports, harbors, creeks, wrecks of the sea, fish royal, deer, wild beasts and fowl, of what nature and kind soever, mines of gold and silver, lead, tin, iron and copper and quarries of stone and coal," together with the royalty of hawking and hunting; reserving however, one-fifth part of all gold mines or gold ore and one-tenth part of all silver mines or silver ore.

Some years after the first grant, Ralph Lord Hopton, John Lord Culpeper, Sir Dudley Wyatt and Thomas Culpeper having died and Lord Hopton having previously sold his interest in these lands to John Trethewey, Esq., the first patent was surrendered in order that a new patent might be granted "with such alterations, provisos and clauses as thereinafter is expressed." Charles thereupon, in the twenty-first year of his reign, being the year 1669, made a new grant of the same territory to Henry Earl of St. Albans, John Lord Berkeley, Sir William Morton and John Tretheway, with the same privileges and the same reservation of rent but with additional powers "to divide the said tract or territory of land into counties, hundreds, parishes, tithings, townships, hamlets, and boroughs, and to erect and build cities, towns, parish churches, colleges, chapels, free schools, alms houses, and houses of correction, and to endow the same, at their free wills and pleasures; and did appoint them full and perpetual patrons of all such churches so to be built and endowed, with power of electing, nominating and presenting, any fit person to the office and place of master of any college or schoolmaster of any school, so to be founded and endowed; with power also to divide any part or parcels of said tract or territory, or portion of lands, into manors, and to call the same after their own or any of their names, or by other name or names whatsoever, and within the same to hold a court, in the nature of a court baron, and to hold pleas of all actions, trespasses, covenants, accounts, contracts, detinues, debts, and demands whatsoever, where the debt or thing demanded exceed not the value of forty shillings of current money of England, and to receive and take all americaments, fines, commodities, advantages, perquisites, and emoluments, whatsoever, to such respective court barons belonging, or in anywise appertaining: And further, to hold within the said manors a court leet, and view of frank pledge, of all the tenants, residents and inhabitants, of the hundreds within such respective manors, to be holden twice in every year, and to erect fairs, markets, courts of pipowder, with all things incident thereto; and to erect parks for breeding, feeding and sustentation of deer, and other wild beasts of chase, etc., etc." This grant was, however, encumbered with a proviso to the effect that such of the land as was not "possessed, inhabited, or planted, by the means or procurement of the said patentees, their heirs or assigns," within the space of twenty-one years, should be forfeited. Later the patentees under this grant sold the "whole tract, territory and portion of land" to Thomas, Lord Culpeper, eldest son and heir of John, late Lord Culpeper.

Thomas, Lord Culpeper, who thus acquired title to the Northern Neck, had, with the Earl of Arlington in 1673 received from Charles a grant of the entire colony of Virginia for thirty-one years, with privileges that practically converted that colony into a proprietary government. This action on the part of the Crown had naturally been resented by the colonists, and commissioners were sent to England to make a vigorous protest. The King, on hearing the case, admitted the justice of these claims, but a settlement of the matter was delayed for various causes, and in 1679, Lord Culpeper, still high in royal favor, was appointed Governor of Virginia. This office, however, he administered in a manner that pleased neither the King nor the people of the colony, and in 1684 he was removed. The way was then opened to an annulment of the grant of 1673 and Lord Culpeper was eventually induced to relinquish all proprietary claims under this grant in exchange for an annual pension from the Crown of six hundred pounds for a period of twenty years. The King in 1688 (James II, in the fourth year of his reign), by way of further compensation confirmed him in possession of the Northern Neck, the lands being relieved under this patent of the proviso as to their settlement within the space of twenty-one years, but the privileges, powers, reservations of rent, etc., remained the same as in the grant to the Earl of St. Albans and others in 1669.

Upon the death of Thomas, Lord Culpeper in 1689, the Northern Neck descended to Alexander Culpeper and from him to Thomas, 6th Lord Fairfax, the son of Lord Culpeper's only daughter, Catherine. In an act of Assembly passed in 1736, this Lord Fairfax is described as the heir-at-law of Thomas, Lord Culpeper and the sole proprietor of the territory included in Lord Culpeper's grant. In this act it was declared "that from henceforth all and every grant and grants, heretofore duly and regularly made and passed by any of the agents or attornies of the Proprietors of the said territory, or any of them, shall be good, available and binding in law, to pass such estate or estates as therein have been granted," and that the grantees should be confirmed in the peaceable possession of the premises granted to them.

In the meantime, Lord Fairfax upon coming into his great inheritance "made a voyage to Virginia to examine his domain". So well pleased was he with the climate and mode of life, that he resolved, after going back to England and arranging his affairs, to return and spend his days amidst this wild territory. About the year 1736 he opened an "office" at Belvoir, in the County of Fairfax, for granting out the land.

The colonial government had, as early as 1730, made grants of land in the Northern Neck west of the Blue Ridge, to Joist Hite and others, aggregating 140,000 acres. Fairfax claimed that these lands were included in his inheritance and appealed to the King. Commissioners were appointed and in 1745, the King in Council, issued an order that the true boundaries of the grant to Lord Culpeper "began at the head spring of the south branch of the Rappahannock which is declared to be that branch of the Rappidan called the "Conway", (for many years the river we know today as the Rappahannock was known as "Hedgman's River") thence northwest in a straight line to the head spring of the Potomac, called "Cohongoroota," the other boundaries being the rivers themselves as they run to the Chesapeake." These boundaries were confirmed by the Virginia

Assembly in 1748. The Northern Neck of Virginia thus defined "included the immense territory now comprising the counties of Lancaster, Northumberland, Richmond, Westmoreland, Stafford, King George, Prince William, Fairfax, Loudoun, Fauquier, Culpeper, Arlington (including the City of Alexandria), Clarke, Madison, Page, Shenandoah, Hardy, Hampshire, Morgan, Berkeley, Jefferson and Frederick."

A few years after his arrival in Virginia, Lord Fairfax had removed to the County of Frederick, built a house which he called "Greenway Court", and there spent the remainder of his life. He was the early patron of George Washington, whom he employed in 1748 to survey and parcel out his lands. Lord Fairfax, it is said, took to his bed when the tidings of the surrender of Lord Cornwallis reached him, and died 9 December 1781.

Before Thomas, 6th Lord Fairfax settled in the colony of Virginia, and during the ownership of his grandmother Culpeper and mother, Catherine, Lady Fairfax, the affairs of the Northern Neck had been run by a series of "resident agents", most notably was Robert "King" Carter of "Corotoman" who lived on the Rappahannock River in Lancaster County. Carter had been granting land on the north side of the north fork of the Rappahannock River beyond Deep Run in what is now Fauquier County since 1706, but usually to political associates like Philip Ludwell, or his own relatives, as his son Charles Carter, who was, when he was granted a large tract of land in 1709, only two years old! There had been some scare of trouble with Indians in the area, but very little, which was erased by the Treaty of Albany in 1722. Carter was able, after this date, to make a good showing by a sudden spate of land grants beyond what had previously been the outermost limits of the frontier.

There had been a settlement on Elk Run in the southern part of what is now Fauquier County before 1723. From it, and from other parts the surveyors followed the stream beds north and west toward Ashby's Bent (now called Gap) in the Blue Ridge Mountains. The old Indian trails had followed the streams, where the going was easier and there was certainty of water. One of these avenues was Cedar Run. Another was Broad Run.

The County Surveyor of Stafford County, of which Fauquier was then a part, was James Thomas; but the man most familiar with the part of the county in which we are interested was John Warner, born and educated in England, who came to Virginia about 1720. He had surveyed for himself in 1731 a patent which adjoined the earlier O'Bannon grant, which Warner later sold to John Peyton. The first Englishman to apply for a grant on Broad Run was Captain William Russell. Captain Russell had many grants in the Northern Neck, more than he could possibly use himself — he was speculating. His grant of 643 acres, dated 17 November 1725, he later sold to John Toward, a keeper of an ordinary in lower Stafford County.

West of Broad Run and north of the Rappahannock Mountain is a broad area of gently rolling and fertile farmland drained by the Piney Branch of Broad Run and Horner's Branch of Carter's Run which flows west of the mountain. 2,823 acres of this choice land (later discovered to be more than 3,000 acres) was patented 10 July 1727 by "Mr." Alexander Scott, Rector of Overwharton Parish. It was in both Stafford and King George Counties. The drainage ridge, which formed, by definition, the line between the two counties ran between Piney Branch, which eventually reached the Potomac, and Horner's Branch which reaches the Rappahannock by way of Carter's Run.

"Mr." Scott was, in fact, the Reverend Alexander Scott, but his ecclesiastical duties did not prevent his being one of the Northern Neck's shrewdest and most active speculators in Proprietary land. He lived at "Dipple", his estate on the Potomac River near Dumfries and seldom, if ever, visited his western land holdings. He died in 1738 leaving his immense estate to his brother, the Reverend James Scott, later Rector of Dettingen Parish.

BRYAN O'BANNON

The first to apply for a grant in the Broad Run Valley with the avowed intention of living on his land was Bryan O'Bannon. His grant, dated 26 June 1728, was first made to one Thomas Jarmyn, of whom we have no further knowledge. Apparently he could not raise the "composition", a fee charged by the Proprietor's office for entering the grant. Bryan O'Bannon was an Irishman, who, according to family tradition, came to Virginia about 1702. It is said, also family tradition, that he "landed in Harper's Ferry", which, anyone knowing the geography and history of Virginia, is ridiculous — unless he came by balloon or UFO!

The O'Bannons were an ancient Irish family, claiming descent from Brian Boru, King of Munster in the tenth century. It is doubtful that such a claim could be proven today but there is a pile of stone on the River Shannon said to be Brougal Castle, built in the 2nd century (?) and occupied by the O'Bannon until the 17th century. It is also said that Bryan O'Bannon's full name was Bryan Boru O'Bannon. If so, it does not appear in any extant record. Another castle, near the River Shannon, in County Offaly, known as Leap Castle is said to be connected to the O'Bannon family.

Again relying on family tradition, Bryan O'Bannon is supposed to have been born in Ireland in 1683. He first settled in Westmoreland County in Virginia and, presumably, married there, but the surname of his wife is unknown. He is referred to as "Bryant Obaning of the County of Westmoreland" when he bought 300 acres in Hanover Parish, Richmond County, 20 December 1720, from Linsfield and John Sharpe. This land, now in Stafford County on the Rappahannock River "about six miles above the falls thereof," he still owned at the time of his death. Presumably he continued to live there several years after his grant of land in Fauquier County, but he was certainly in Fauquier County before 1741 when he received another grant of land adjoining the first one.

Bryan O'Bannon had six children, three boys and three girls. The eldest, Catherine, was born in 1708 and married Jacob Hite, son of Yoist Hite, a pioneer Shenandoah Valley settler, whom we met earlier. The eldest son, John, born about 1710, married Sarah Barbee, daughter of Thomas Barbee of Stafford County. William O'Bannon, the next son, was born about 1713. About 1735 he married Elizabeth Duncan, a widow with two children, Joseph and Catherine Duncan. Next came Samuel O'Bannon, born 1715. It is believed that he married (1) Judith Sharpe and (2) Elizabeth ____. The next child was Anne, who, for reasons not quite clear, is referred to as Mary in the settlement of her father's estate. She married Simon Miller. The other child was Elizabeth, who married (1) John Ambrose and (2) John Etherington.

The O'Bannon patent of 1728 almost totally encompasses the area known as the Great Meadow today. It lies on both sides of Broad Run between Routes 698 and 245. The present Route 17 approximates its western boundary but there are small bits west and north of both Route 17 and 245. These fragments have, throughout the years, almost always been in controversy. It is not possible to determine the limits of the patent simply by the description in the Northern Neck Grants as issued by the Proprietor's office. As is true in many instances, the O'Bannon heirs and those who purchased land from the O'Bannon estate, claimed an area considerably in excess of the

635 acres called for in the grant. In fact, by computation today, the total was more nearly 1,085 acres, an excess of 450 acres.

The first grant contained a relatively small area south of Broad Run. On the 19th of June, 1741, Bryan O'Bannon was granted another 197 acres south of Broad Run cornering on the "poison field" mentioned in the grant to John Toward and adjoining his first grant. On this tract of land together with that part of the first tract south of the run, he created what is called in his will "the plantation whereon I now live." No vestige of the house in which he lived has been found, so we know only that he lived between Broad Run and the Pignut Mountain, the slope of which nearly touches the southeast boundary of his land.

That Bryan O'Bannon remained in King George County until his second grant, or just before receiving it, seems to be verified by his activity there prior to 1741. In December, 1727 he acted as a bondsman for Adam Christy on the estate of William Pattishall, in which estate he was paid a sum of money. In 1733 he acted as an appraiser of the estate of Thomas Philips, deceased along with Linefield Sharp and in 1736 in the same capacity for the estate of Richard Gill, deceased. The three appraisers of the estate of Thomas Phillips lived in upper Brunswick Parish in what is now Stafford County.

Bryan O'Bannon wrote his will on the 4th of September 1760. His wife was dead and his estate was given to his six children, except for 150 acres he had taken up in Frederick County which he left to Aaron and Francis Johnston, children of Margaret Johnston and presumably himself, out of wedlock. His daughter Catherine is not mentioned, although his son-in-law, Catherine's husband, Jacob Hite, is appointed to look after the Johnson children. All of the land went to his sons. The youngest, Samuel, was given the 300 acres in King George County. However, even before Bryan O'Bannon's will was submitted for probate, Samuel sold the land he received under it — he being at that time of Johnson County, North Carolina. He sold the 300 acres in Brunswick Parish, King George County, to Esdras Edzard, 15 October 1762. (King George Co., DB 4, p. 500).

The land on Broad Run was left to Bryan O'Bannon's two older sons, John and William, and their eldest sons, Thomas son of John, and William, son of William, in four almost equal parcels. Bryan O'Bannon had hardly gone to his rest when his two grandsons, William and Thomas, decided to sell the land he had left them. In July 1762 William O'Bannon sold 50 acres at the north end of his dividend to his kinsman, Alexander Farrow. (Alexander Farrow had married Ann O'Bannon, whose parentage has not been established. She was thought to have been Mary Ann O'Bannon, daughter of Bryan and to have been married, first, to Alexander Farrow and, second, to Simon Miller. Farrow and wife sold property to O'Bannon on 3 June 1766, witnessed by Simon Miller. Simon Miller died in 1770, making a total of four years in which Simon Miller became a grandfather — he left his property to his grandchildren, the children of his daughter Elizabeth. This would have been impossible.) The tract sold to Alexander Farrow was clearly beyond the northernmost limits of his grandfather's patent, but was south of the Grinnan patent ('Gordonsdale') then owned by the Scott heirs. It was approximately at the point where the present Route 17 meets Route 245 and probably included the ground on which Lawrence's Tavern was later built. About one year later William O'Bannon sold Farrow the remainder of the land left him by his grandfather, making a total of 306 acres, about 100 acres more than was granted him in the will. The tract reached from present Route 245 south to Route 698. In 1766 Farrow sold both tracts back to John O'Bannon, Sr.

Thomas O'Bannon sold his 220 acres to Samuel Rust 29 June 1763. The tract was south of Broad Run and Route 698 and had been part of his grandfather's home plantation, although the house was not on it.

Bryan O'Bannon left "to Each my Grand Children both Male & Female being twenty-seven in Number the sum of Ten pounds Current Each .." His will was proved by oath of the witnesses, Elias Edmonds, Sam'l. Earle and Jas. Rogers, on 25 February 1762. The inventory of his personal estate totalled £863.6.2. (Fauq. Co. Will Book 1, pp. 41-43 and pp. 48-50).

<u>ISSUE (O'BANNON)</u>:

+ 2.   Catherine[2], b. 1708; d. 1766
+ 3.   John[2], b. 1710; d. 1774
+ 4.   William[2], b. 1712;
+ 5.   Mary Anne[2], b. 1718; d.
+ 6.   Samuel[2], b. 1715; d.
+ 7.   Elizabeth[2], b.   ; d. 1777

SECOND GENERATION

2. CATHERINE[2] O'BANNON (Bryan[1]) married Jacob Hite, son of Yoist Hite, pioneer Shenandoah Valley settler. Cartmell, in his "Shenandoah Valley Pioneers" and repeated in du Bellet's "Some Prominent Virginia Families", states that Jacob Hite and Catherine O'Bannon were married in Dublin, Ireland. It is stated that Jacob, who owned an interest in his father's brigantine <u>Swift</u>, had met Catherine on one of his voyages to Ireland. There is some doubt as to the dates of birth of both Catherine (the date of her birth and those of the other children of Bryan being taken from the records of the late Walter O'Bannon of Tulsa, Oklahoma) and Jacob Hite. If they were married in Dublin, it is quite possible that at the same time Jacob brought his bride home to Virginia he transported her father, Bryan, and the rest of the family. Jacob Hite moved to South Carolina, with his second wife and children, and was massacred by Indians.

ISSUE (HITE):

+ 8.   John[3], b.   ;d. 1777
+ 9.   Thomas[3], b. 1750; d. 1776
  10.   Jacob O'Bannon[3], killed by Indians, 1778
+ 11.   Mary[3]
+ 12.   Elizabeth[3]

3. JOHN[2] O'BANNON (Bryan[1]) married Sarah, the daughter of Thomas and Margaret Barbee of Stafford County prior to 1748, perhaps many years, as she was Thomas Barbee's eldest child. According to his father's will (1762) he received the following: the plantation and land whereon he now lives containing 212 acres and Negro woman Judy and after the death of John and Sarah, his wife, to go to John's daughter Sarah. On 2 June 1766 John (called John O'Bannon, Sen'r. of the Parish of Hamilton) bought two tracts of land from Alexander Farrow, viz: Pignut Ridge on Broad Run and "Waggon Road at head of Carter's Run." On 22 October 1770 he sold 100 acres of the tract on Pignut Ridge, bounded by Waggon Road, Chapman and Scott, to James Nelson. This acreage was located on the northwest corner of what is now Great Meadow. John O'Bannon was appointed to the first vestry of Leeds Parish when it was formed from Hamilton Parish in 1769. His will, made 18 November 1773 and proved 28 March 1774, is recorded in Fauquier County Will Book 1, pp. 237-239.

ISSUE (O'BANNON):

+ 13.   John[3], b: 1735; d: 1797
+ 14.   Sarah[3], b: 1737; d:
  15.   Thomas[3], b: 1739; d:
+ 16.   James[3], b: 1741; d: 1808
+ 17.   William[3], b: d: 1807
+ 18.   Andrew[3], b: 1745; d: 1813
+ 19.   George[3], b: ; d: 1777
+ 20.   Caty[3]

+ 21. Joseph[3]
+ 22. Bryant[3], b: 1750; d: 1784
+ 23. Benjamin[3], b: 1759; d: 1839
+ 24. Samuel[3], b: 1751; d: 1822

4. WILLIAM[2] O'BANNON (Bryan[1]) married Elizabeth Duncan, widow, about 1735. She had a son, Joseph Duncan, and a daughter, Catherine Duncan, who was named in the will of William's sister, Elizabeth O'Bannon Etherington (or Edrington) in 1776. Whether or not William was married previously is not known. On 27 Sept. 1764 (Fauquier County) Wm. O'Bannon and wife Elizabeth recorded a deed of gift, for love and affection, to Joseph Duncan for 50 acres. Joseph W. Duncan married Hannah Jennings after 1788, sister of Fannie Jennings, wife of Thomas O'Bannon, one of the witnesses to this deed, and a nephew of William. Neither a will nor administration has been found for William O'Bannon. It is not known where, nor when, he died, but he died after 1763 when his son signed the deed to land left him by his grandfather Bryan. (DeHuff, p. 47)

ISSUE (O'BANNON):

+ 25. William[3]
+ 26. Elizabeth[3]
+ 27. Bryant[3]
+ 28. Mildred[3]
+ 29. John[3]
+ 29a. Catherine[3]

5. MARY ANNE[2] O'BANNON (Bryan[1]) married Simon Miller. He made his will on 26 March 1769 and was proved on 26 Febr. 1770. (Fq. Co. W. B. 1, pp. 155-156). It has been suggested that Mary Anne O'Bannon had married, first, Alexander Farrow; however this could not have been possible as Alexander Farrow was still living in 1766 and Simon Miller left his property to his grandchildren, children of his daughter Elizabeth, thought to have been the only child of Simon and Mary Anne (O'Bannon) Miller. To have become a grandfather in four years would have been quite a feat!

ISSUE (MILLER):

+ 30. Elizabeth[3]

6. SAMUEL[2] O'BANNON (Bryan[1]) married Judith Sharpe. Samuel inherited his father's plantation in King George County, consisting of 300 acres. To this Bryan added £100 and all his wearing apparel. Shortly after Bryan's death Samuel migrated to North Carolina where, on 15 Oct. 1762, he deeded his 300 acres in Brunswick Parish to Esdras Edzard of King George (K.G. D.B.

4, p. 500; rec: 2 Dec. 1762). The conveyances of lease and release describe the land as "being in the parish of Brunswick and County of King George above the falls of Rapp'k River being part or parcell of Twelve hundred & Fifty acres of Land formerly grant to Thos. Knight .. 5 June 1704 the one of which Joins to Lincefield Sharpe .." and another side to John Sharpe. The "release", following the "lease" is dated 16 October, between "Samuel Obannon of North Carolina in Johnston County planter," and Edzard. After Samuel's signature is a curious notation: "The words & Eliz: his wife in the second line & Frances his wife in the third line & Eliz: his wife in the forth line & them in the fifth line .." suggest that Samuel had remarried to Elizabeth _?_ . She did not join him in conveying the property. Someone writing to the O'BANNON GENEALOGIST, Vol. 1, No. 2, p. 29, suggests that Samuel had more children than just Thomas (of whom later) and named possibly a son Bryan and a daughter Ann, who might have been the wife of Alexander Farrow. Samuel accumulated some property in Johnston Co., N. C. which he sold and disappeared from the records. (See: DeHuff, p. 15f)

ISSUE (O'BANNNON):

31.   Thomas[3] — the descendants of Thomas O'Bannon, b: 1738; d: 1801, are given in a printed pamphlet, "The Family of Thomas O'Bannon of Fauquier County, Virginia and Barnwell County, South Carolina" by Elizabeth Willis DeHuff, Augusta, Ga. (1969).

7. ELIZABETH[2] O'BANNON (Bryan[1]) married, first, John Ambrose and, 2nd, John Etherington (sometimes spelled Edrington) in Fauquier County on 29 November 1762. The bondsman was Augustine Jennings. Elizabeth died, testate, in Fauquier County in 1778. Her will, dated 29 November 1776 was proved on 23 March 1778. She left "to my beloved nephew Thomas Obannon, son to Samuel Obannon, one still", one negroe Woman named Luse .. Negroe man named Harry .. negroe man named Tom. "I also give all my goods & chattels to my beloved nephew .." (Fq. Co. W.B. 1, pp. 323-324). The evaluation of her personal estate amounting to £933.3.6 was returned on 24 August 1778.

****

The Second Generation, the grandchildren of Bryan O'Bannon, number 24, possibly 25, in the account given above. Somewhere there are two or three missing, if according to Bryan's will he had at his death in 1762, 27 grandchildren.

THIRD GENERATION

8. JOHN[3] HITE (Catherine[2] Bryan[1]) married Sarah Nichols of Baltimore. They lived in Winchester, VA. He died 1777.

ISSUE (HITE):

32.   Mary[4] , m. 25 May 1797, Edward Gault
33.   Sarah[4], m. 14 Jan. 1794, Alexander Pelt Buchanan.
34.   Catherine[4], m. 20 April 1793, Theodoric Lee, son of Henry and Lucy (Grimes) Lee and grandson of Richard Lee.

9. THOMAS[3] HITE (Catherine[2]) married 10 November 1772, Frances Madison Beale, b. 1 October 1749, dau. of his stepmother, Mrs. Frances Beale, nee Madison, by her first marriage.

ISSUE (HITE):

35.   Frances Madison[4], b.   d. 1851.
36.   James[4], b. 6 Oct. 1776; d.

11. MARY[3] HITE (Catherine[2]) married (1st) The Rev. Nathaniel Manning; m. (2nd) The Rev. Mr. Busby.

12. ELIZABETH[3] HITE (Catherine[2]) married Tavenner Beale, Jr., son of her stepmother, by her first marriage.

ISSUE (BEALE):

37.   John[4]
38.   Charles[4]
39.   Thomas[4]
40.   James Madison Hite[4]
41.   Catherine[4]
42.   Elizabeth[4]
43.   Mary[4]

13. JOHN[3] O'BANNON (John[2], Bryan[1]) was born ca. 1735, the son of John and Sarah (Barbee) O'Bannon. He married, probably in Prince William County, VA., Lydia (Duncan) Stamps, dau. of Joseph Duncan and widow of Thomas Stamps, Jr. On 22 Nov. 1756, she was appointed administrator of the estate of her dead husband by the County Court of Prince William County (Order Book 1755-57, p. 239). There is no marriage bond recorded in Fauquier County for Capt.

John O'Bannon and Lydia Stamps. By her first marriage Lydia had two known children, viz: 1) Molly Stamps, who married 27 Dec. 1788, Simon Matthew. Wm. Stamps, bondsman to the marriage bond. They were married by Elder Robert Sanders of Broad Run Baptist Church; 2) Hannah Stamps, m: Richard Keeble (or Kibble) In 1807 Lydia O'Bannon gave her daugher a "negro boy named Benjamin .." Richard Keeble died, testate, in Fauquier Co.; his will being probated on 28 April 1812. (W. B. 5, p. 260)

After the Revolution many of the O'Bannons sold whatever inheritances they had and moved from Fauquier, lured by visions of a more abundant life in Kentucky. It is difficult to determine the route they took to the "dark and bloody ground", whether by the Cumberland Gap, through southwest Virginia, or across the mountain to the Monongahela and thus to the Ohio River, where they bought rafts to take them down the river to the Promised Land.

Captain John O'Bannon elected to stay in Fauquier. After the war he acquired,by inheritance and purchase from several of his relatives who were headed west, a large estate comprising most of the southern part of his grandfather's original patents and several adjacent tracts from the Byrum and Peyton patents.

John O'Bannon was a Captain in the Fauquier Militia, his commission predated 1776. He was recommended to Governor Thomas Jefferson to be commissioned Major by a petition of 11 fellow officers of the Fauquier Militia; he having served as Captain the longest of any of the appointed officers. It is not know what the Governor's decision to this petition was. He died in 1797, leaving his Fauquier County land (some 849 acres) and large land bountys in Kentucky secured for service in the Revolution to six sons, subject to the life interest of his wife Lydia. (W.B. 3, pp. 52-56) Before his land in Fauquier County could be divided, after the death of Lydia (Duncan) O'Bannon about 1811, four of his sons were in Kentucky, one had died and only one, Joseph, was in Fauquier County. Not even he remained in the Broad Run Valley, but moved to property near The Plains, where he died in 1824.

Captain John O'Bannon left his son William, 283 acres on the top of the Pignut Mountain, most of which was from the original patent of Peter Byrum which he had picked up from the Eustace heirs. William O'Bannon already owned adjoining land, having acquired most of Brian O'Bannon's second patent of 1741 from William Asbury in 1797. (FCD.B. 12, 121)

Capt. O'Bannon's estate, at the time of his death, was appraised at £3710.6.9 1/2. In 1811 the personal estate was divided and in 1816 the real estate was divided.

ISSUE (O'BANNON):

+ 44.   Joseph[4], b: 1759; d: 1824
+ 45.   Elizabeth[4]
+ 46.   James[4], b: 1764; d: May 1850 (Henry Co., KY.)
+ 47.   Jemima[4], b: 1767; d: 30 Nov. 1786.
+ 48.   Isham[4]
+ 49.   Elias[4], b: ; d: July 1828.
+ 50.   John[4], b: Feb. 1773; d: bef. 1816
+ 51.   William[4]

14. SARAH[3] O'BANNON (John[2], Bryan[1]) Sarah married, 25 June 1765, James Foley, in Fauquier County. She inherited from her father "one negroe boy named Will, now in her possession." She died before 1786, at which time license was issued to James Foley to marry Elizabeth Oglesby (Ogilvie). It is not known if James Foley was married prior to Sarah O'Bannon. However, James' daughter mentioned in his will (W.B. 3, p. 51, proved 24 April 1797) was married after license was issued, 16 Oct. 1777, Fauquier County, to Francis Watts. She (Sarah Foley) would have been only 11 years old at the most, if she were Sarah's daughter. James' will, dated 14 Oct. 1793 and proved 24 April 1797, divided his children by his wife Elizabeth Ogilivie by giving their children his wife's maiden name, viz: Susanna Foley Oglevie, Presley Foley Oglivie, Leah Foley Oglivie. More proof of relationship is given by the widow's division and allotment (W.B. 5, p. 294), proved 23 Febr. 1809. Dr. Chandler Peyton, William O'Bannon and Walter A. Smith were appointed Comm'rs. to divide the land of Elizabeth Foley, dec'd, in three equal parts: one to Susanna W. Foley, one to Presley Foley and one to Elias Mathew in right of his wife, Leah. The Foley family lived on the slopes of the Pignut Mountain, just north of the O'Bannon family.

ISSUE (FOLEY):

52.   Enoch[4], m: Polly Eskridge, 15 June 1801 (Fauq. Co.)
53.   Lettice[4], m; Benjamin Duncan, 13 Sept. 180_
54.   Molley[4] (or Polly), m: Taliaferro Ball, 18 April 1807.
55.   John[4]
56.   James[4]
57.   Thomas[4]
58.   William[4], m: Mary Feagins, 23 July 1783
+ 59.   Sarah[4], m: Francis Watts
60.   Bryant[4], m: Elizabeth West, 30 July 1808; d:, testate, in Fauquier County, 1811.

16. JAMES[3] O'BANNON (John[2], Bryan[1]) was born in 1741 in Fauquier County, VA. and died 1809 in Washington County, KY. He was drowned in the Rolling Fork River. He married Mary Mason, about whom very little or nothing is known, nor the date of their marriage. James had received from his father "a good suit cloths to be purchased out of my crop." This seems very little to have

received from the landed John O'Bannon, however, he was referred to as "my loving son James." Possibly his father had advanced him money and therefore had no claim upon the estate. In 1779 he received a grant from Lord Fairfax in the Northern Neck Proprietary for 99 acres in Shenandoah County, VA. The property was located in "Powells Big Fort" on Passage Creek. The yearly rent was one shilling, sterling. This property he sold to Charles Murphy on 29 Sept. 1788 (Shen. Co. D.B. G-H, p. 435). Powell's Fort Valley is a long, narrow valley secluded in the walls of the Massanutten Mountains which rise between the present day Front Royal and Strasburg and extend south to Harrisonburg. They probably moved to Kentucky the same year they sold the farm. In Lincoln County, KY. Tax List for 1789 the name of James O'Bannon appears. He then moved to Washington County, KY. where his children were beginning to take husbands and wives. There is very little mention of James in the records of Washington County, KY. The inventory and appraisement of his estate is recorded in W.B. B, page 59 (Washington County), returned 9 Oct. 1809.

ISSUE (O'BANNON):

61. Nancy[4], b: 16 Oct. 1772, m: James Coppage in Lincoln County, Kentucky.
62. John[4], b: d: unmarried.
63. Rebecca[4], b: ca: 1774, probably in Shen. County. Married William Ray, 29 Febr. 1795 in Washington Co., KY.
64. Sarah[4], b: ca. 1776, m: Nathaniel Ray, 18 Nov. 1796, Washington Co., KY.
65. Catharine[4], b: ca. 1780 in VA.; m: William Dyer, 25 Dec. 1802 in Washington County.
66. Mary[4] (or Polly), b: Virginia; m: 31 Jan. 1803, Alexander Coppage.
67. James[4], b: VA.; d: 23 April 1855, age 70 years, Cumberland Co., KY. He married 11 March 1809, Elizabeth Bentley, Lincoln Co., KY.
68. William[4], b: ca: 1783; m: Sarah _____. She was born ca. 1794 in Virginia according to the 1850 Census of Cumberland Co., KY.
69. Rhoda[4], b: ca: 1794 in Washington Co., KY. Married 23 Nov. 1815, Cumberland Co., KY., Aquilla Hall (sometimes spelled Equillor). They moved about 1821/23 to Morgan County, IL.
70. Evan[4] (or Even), b: 22 April 1799, Washington Co.,KY. M: (1st) Margaret Hall. They moved to Morgan Co., IL. He m: (2nd) in Adams Co., IL., Mary Cole and m: (3rd) on 7 Sept. 1849 at Kanesville, Pottawattamie, Iowa, Jane Hawley Weatherbee Booth. (She having married twice before. After his death, Jane married William Dickenson Pratt. Evan and Jane (with all the names!) O'Bannon were the great-great grandparents of Mildred Sadie and Melvin Samuel Ames. Mildred (Ames) Vorwaller will be long remembered by genealogists of the O'Bannon family for her work in the records of the family and her short-lived publication, THE O'BANNON GENEALOGIST.
71. Garrett[4], b: ca: 1802, Washington Co., KY. Moved to Cumberland Co., KY. along with his mother, Rhoda and Evan O'Bannon. He must have left KY. about the same time as his brother Evan and sister Rhoda, for he married Patsey Nivens and lived in Morgan Co., IL. After his death she married (2nd) Aaron Thompson and left issue by both marriages.

17. WILLIAM[3] O'BANNON (John[2], Bryan[1]) According to William O'Bannon's tombstone in the O'Bannon-Lawrence Cemetery near the site of his home at Marshall, Fauquier Co., VA., he was born in 1729 and died 19 October 1807. The stone is rough granite with the crude inscription: "W OB, Ano Oct 19 1807 AG 78". He married Ann Neville, dau. of Joseph and Ann (Bohannon) Neville; she died in 1824. When William's father died in 1774 he received a "Plantation and lands on the East Side of Pignut Ridge .. whereon he formerly lived.." This would indicate that William O'Bannon was living on the tract of land at Salem (now Marshall) that was part of the Elias Edmonds tract of 2000 acres, patented by Capt. James Ball of Lancaster County, VA. in 1732. Four hundred acres of this tract was sold by Elias Edmonds to William O'Bannon in 1770, and the rest of the tract was sold to him in two purchases later. The deed, recorded 23 Oct. 1770 (D.B. 4, p. 71) states Elias Edmonds of Parish of Leeds, County of Fauquier .. Gent., & Betty, his wife [William's cousin] to William O'Bannon, Jr. .. £130 .. unto William O'Bannon .. now in his actual possession .. part of tract granted to Capt. James Ball .. commonly called the horspen tract .. corner to John Blowers .. with his line to Col. Thos. Harrison's 400 acres .. together with all houses .. except David Barton's Dwelling house .. Signed: Elias Edmonds, Betty Edmonds. (Betty Edmonds was a daughter of Simon Miller and Mary O'Bannon).

The land that William O'Bannon owned near the present town of Marshall formed a cresent around the small farm owned by Dr. John Monroe. His land extended from the present Trinity Episcopal Church and the Marshall Baptist Church, north to the railroad crossing on Rt. 55 and around the railroad to the Rectortown Road crossing and west to the UtterbackRussell farm, one mile west of Marshall.

On 12 December 1806 William O'Bannon made his will which was probated on 27 October 1807. The provisions of the will are as follows: Wife Ann .. the plantation whereon I now live, and 100 acres of land, a part of the tract I purchased from the Tarflingers joining said plantation and George Elgin's land, also 4 negroes, one old Negro wench named Jim, the waggon and four horses, ten head of choice cattle .. all farming utensils and household and kitchen furniture .. one of the best beds and furniture excepted. Son, William .. 200 acres on the Miami River [Ohio] .. Son, Presley Neville .. one of the best beds and furniture .. son Jesse .. equal part with other children of moveable property to be paid them in clothing .. son, Alexander .. (same as Jesse's) .. Land property to be divided equally between my other children that may be living at the time of my death, William, Jesse and Alexander are to have no part of the land only as above mentioned. After the death of my wife Ann all the above mentioned property given to her or what there may be remaining thereof is to be equally divided between my surviving children, Jesse and Alexander excepted and William is to have no part of the land. He appointed sons Thomas and Joseph and Presley N. O'Bannon as executors with a special charge to Presley Neville to "Pay every possible attention to his mother and see her righted in every instance." On 24 Oct. 1808, Presley N. O'Bannon came into Court and qualified as an executor.

Ann (Neville) O'Bannon died in the year 1824. On 8 Nov. 1824 the Dower Tract on which William O'Bannon, dec'd. lived was divided by the following appointed Commissioners: Joseph Fauntleroy, Edward Shacklett, John Shacklett and Charles Duncan. The land was divided into lots by the above Commissioners as follows: Lot No. 1 .. to Bryant O'Bannon; No. 2 to Thomas

O'Bannon; No. 3 to Agnes Jeffries, wife of George Jeffries; No. 4 to William Utterback, husband of Polly; No. 5 to Joseph O'Bannon; No. 6 to Elijah Pepper, husband of Sally O'Bannon; No. 7 to Presley N. O'Bannon; House Lot to Mason Lawrence, husband of Nancy O'Bannon. The other land of William O'Bannon had been divided in 1813 and consisted of 543½ acres. This was done as follows: Lot No. 1 to John O'Bannon, 66 acres; No. 2 to Elizabeth Pepper, 68 acres; Lot No. 3 to Joseph O'Bannon, 66 acres; No. 4 to Bryant O'Bannon, 62 acres; No. 5 to Mason Lawrence, 64 acres; No. 6 to Children of Joyce Lawrence (she was dead by 1813 and had married John Lawrence, 13 March 1786). Her children were Thomas, Polly, Agatha, Catharine, Peter, John, Sally, and Mason., 62½ acres; No. 7 to George Jeffries, 60 acres. Other tracts: sons Thomas and Presley Neville O'Bannon and son-in-law William Utterback, the farm adjoining Thomas Glascock. Also, sons Thomas and Presley Neville the farm on the south side of Pignut Ridge, adjoining Wm. Skinker. To sons Jesse and Alexander the tract of land adjoining Daniel Flowerree's land — they came for a part of the real estate after all! To son William, land on the Miami River, in Ohio.

The old home of William O'Bannon — he was sometimes referred to as Captain William O'Bannon — stood until the early 1950's when it gradually fell to ruin. It is known locally as "The Lawrence Place". After the death of Mrs. Drucilla (Utterback) Russell, a descendant, the property was sold and the cemetery with its ancient boxwoods and stone wall have been neglected and allowed to become a thicket of briars and honeysuckle.

ISSUE (O'BANNON):

+ 72.   William[4]
+ 73.   Presley Neville[4]
  74.   Jesse[4], purchased on 2 Jan. 1836 one half of a ½-acre lot in Salem (No. 20). He apparently never married, or he died without heirs leaving his estate to his nephew, Wilfred Utterback, to whom he devised the house and lot purchased in 1836. His will was proved in Fauquier County, 28 May 1844 (W.B. 19, p. 25) and was contested by other nephews and nieces, but it was declared legal.
+ 75.   Alexander[4]
+ 76.   Thomas[4]
+ 77.   Joseph[4]
+ 78.   Agnes[4]
+ 79.   Polly[4]
+ 80.   Sally[4] (or Elizabeth)
+ 81.   Nancy[4]
+ 82.   Bryant[4]
+ 83.   Joyce[4]
+ 83a.   John[4]

18. ANDREW[3] O'BANNON (John[2], Bryan[1]) married on 10 October 1777, Mary (Pepper) Smith, widow of Joseph Smith, Jr. and daughter of Samuel and Elizabeth (Holton) Pepper. Andrew was appointed guardian of Ruth, Wilhelmania [sic] and Abner Smith, orphans of Joseph Smith, de'd on

24 Nov. 1777. On 26 Oct. 1789 (October Court) John Smith was appointed gdn. of Abner Smith and the Court ordered William Edmonds, Edward Digges, John Sinclair and John O'Bannon to settle Andrew O'Bannon's account of his guardianship of the orphans and divide the estate. In his father's will Andrew was bequeathed, in lieu of all legacies bequeathed him by his grandfather, Bryan O'Bannon, one negroe man named Frank. Andrew, no doubt, was one of the 27 grandchildren of Bryan who was supposed to have received £10 which John did not deliver to him. Andrew enlisted in the Army in 1776/7 under Captain John Chilton and marched under Colonel Thomas Marshall, in the 3rd Virginia Regiment, from Fauquier County to the North and was Waggon Master of the Regiment. He was the owner of a wagon and team employed in the service and lost both by capture. He was in the Army during the battles of Germantown, Monmouth and Brandywine. His Captain, John Chilton, was killed at Brandywine.

Andrew O'Bannon had a lease on the Rappahannock Mountain, near the present town of The Plains, above the Old Tavern, from George William Fairfax, Esq., dated 23 August 1787, for 150 acres. This was Lot #16 of 2,655 acres. The lease was taken out for a period "during the natural lives of Andrew O'Bannon, Molley O'Bannon, his wife and William Barby O'Bannon their son .. rent three pounds 16 shillings."

Mary (Pepper) (Smith) O'Bannon, wife of Andrew, was married, first, to Joseph Smith, Jr., son of Captain Joseph Smith (1718-1793) and wife, Katherine Anderson, of "Mt. Eccentric". "Mt. Eccentric" was an early Smith home on a slope of the Pignut Mt., near the O'Bannon family lands. Joseph and Mary (Pepper) Smith had three children, as mentioned above,viz: 1) Ruth, b: 10 March 1772, m: 4 April ___ John Logan, in Mason Co., Ky.; 2) Wilhemina (Milly), b: ca: 1773, m: 23 October 1797, Joseph Burdett; 3) Abner Smith, b: ca: 1775; m: (1st) 24 Jan. 1802, Nancy Jennings, in Shenandoah County, Va.; the records show that he was married a second time. One record says that he was a doctor.

Wilhelmina Smith had married her first cousin, Joseph Burdett, in 1797 in Fauquier County and shortly thereafter, probably after the settlement of Wilhemina's father's estate, moved to Garrard Co., Ky. It seems that Andrew and Mary (Pepper) O'Bannon also moved to Garrard County at the same time. Mary died sometime after 25 Dec. 1837 when she made her will in Garrard County.

ISSUE (O'BANNON):

84. Elijah[4], b: 1785; d: 1868
85. Elizabeth[4], m: Henry Kemper and left issue.
86. Daniel[4] d: 1849
87. Mary (Polly)[4]
88. Yelverton[4,] b: 1794; d: 1834
89. William Barbee[4], d: ca: 1828; m. 1806 Susan Thompson. Lived in Fleming Co., Ky.

19. GEORGE[3] O'BANNON (John[2], Bryan[1]) was a member of Capt. John Ashby's Company, 3rd Virginia Regiment, and was killed in New York at the Battle of Haarlem in 1777. Several members of the company had written wills, one, at least, is recorded in Fauquier, other than George O'Bannon's. His will was a letter he had written to his mother on the eve of battle. The letter is recorded in Fauquier County W. B. l, pp. 311-312. For further reading on the Battle of the Heights of Haarlem and George's involvement, see: FAUQUIER COUNTY IN THE REVOLUTION.

> "Dear mother and brothers i writ to let you know that i am in good health thanks be to God for it at this present hoping this lines will find you all in health. Remember me to all my frends not forgetting Cuzzen Elizzabeth Barbe remember my love to her. I don't expect that i shall write any more and to let you know that wey are not ben in know battle yet but we yerepect it every day and night wey are on a iland we have know way to get off we must fit our way off our men is a fiting every day and night. the other night a battle the nue yourke iland other night at kings bridge wrothe Town is on the Island i am in grat hopes that i shawl see you all again but we expect a battle evere day and night i am gart hops that the town will be burnt in a few days the English wod have burnt it before this time but they want the town for barracks but if they dont burn the Town we Shawll burn the town our slves now more at present but your dutiful son. George Obannon. it is my desire that my brother Benjamin Obannon should have all my estat after my dets is paid i hope my der brothers you wont think amiss of it for i think he want it worse after my death."

The letter arrived home and was presented to the Court for probate on 25 August 1777, the handwriting being sworn to as George's by oaths of James Foley, Jun'r. A Certicate was granted to Joseph Nelson.

20. CATY[3] O'BANNON (John[2], Bryan[1]) m: (as his first wife), Joseph Nelson, on 23 Dec. 1771, Fauquier Co., Va. She was born ca. 1751. Joseph Nelson was appointed as an Ensign in the Fauquier County militia and took the oath as such 22 May 1780. He was discharged from active service on 9 Sept. 1781 and was the recipient of a Revolutionary War Pension. He was married twice, after the death of Caty (or Catherine) and died in Fauquier Co., intestate, 6 Oct. 1837. It is believed that Joseph Nelson was buried on "the old Tom Courtney place" in Carter's run valley — now owned by Irving Ashby (1991). (Information from: Bradshaw, J. D.: THE WIGFIELD AND NELSON FAMILIES OF FAUQUIER CO., VIRGINIA ... (Richmond, 1986)

ISSUE (NELSON):

90.   John B.[4], b: 29 Sept. 1772; d: 22 Feb. 1847, Cooper Co., Mo. M: 14 Sept. 1798, Fauq. Co., Cynthia Ann Withers.

91.   James O'Bannon[4], b: ca: 1774; d: unm: 23 May 1813, Fauq.

92.   Thomas Henry[4], b: 14 Dec. 1777; m: 2 Nov. 1802, Elizabeth Green, Fauq. Co. He d: 21 Dec. 1856.

93.   Joseph, Jr[4], b: ca: 1778; m: 28 Dec. 1803, Nancy Rosser, Fauq. Co.

94.   George[4], b: 7 July 1786; m: 15 July 1815, Elizabeth Hord Porter, Fauquier County, Va.

95. Nancy[4], b: 1788, m: (1st) Enoch Withers, 15 July 1815, Fauq. Co. She m: (2nd) Fielding Templeman (no issue) Had by first marriage: (WITHERS) 1) James O'B., 1804-1847. 2) Thornton, 1807-1878. Nancy[4] died in 1845.

21. JOSEPH[3] O'BANNON (John[2], Bryan[1]) married Abagail (_____) Giles, widow of John Giles, who died in jail in 1781. She is mentioned in "Women of the American Revolution", as Abrigail O'Bannon. Abigail O'Bannon, Winton Co., S.C. was executrix for John Giles, dec'd, late of Camden. Signed power of attorney to Joseph O'Bannon to collect indent due John Giles for services under Frederick Kimball. Joseph signed one receipt. He purchased many parcels of property in South Carolina. In 1785, he purchased 150 acres in Orangeburg District on waters of Gant of "Little Salt Kitchey." Other property was 465 acres in 96 District; 127 acres in 96 District; 246 acres in Winton Co. (now Barnwell Co.) S.C. Witness to this property was Thomas O'Bannon and William Hardin.

There are deeds of sale in Greenville Co., S.C. from Joseph and Abigail. They moved to Barren Co., Ky. before 1800 when they begin to appear on Tax Lists and the 1810 Census. He must have died some time between 1811 and 1813 when Abby O'Bannon is listed with three horses and H. James O'Bannon and Joseph O'Bannon, Jr. with one horse each.

ISSUE (O'BANNON):

96. Joseph[4]
97. H. James[4]
98. Betsy[4] probably the Betsy who m: 1808 _____ Hawkins.
99. Elias[4], of the 1850 Census, Crawford Co., Ind. thought to be a son of Joseph. Possibly others.

22. BRYANT[3] O'BANNON (John[2], Bryan[1]) married Elizabeth ____. He died in Berkeley County, Va. (now W. Va.) in 1784, leaving widow Elizabeth and a son John named in his will in Norborne Parish, dated 19 April 1784; proved 15 June 1784. He bequeathed one-half of his lands to son John O'Bannon and stated that if son John should die, the land was to be given to his (Bryant's) brother Samuel and Samuel's son Enoch. (W. B. 1, p. 356). This will appears in the Court Records in Augusta County "McCormick vs. O'Bannon". Bryant O'Bannon possibly had a posthumous son Bryant O'Bannon (Gdn. Accounts, 18 Dec. 1793).

ISSUE (O'BANNON):

100. John[4], b: 1755;
101. Bryant[4] (thought to have lived later in Kentucky)

23. BENJAMIN[3] O'BANNON (John[2], Bryan[1]) married Eleanor Ash, Fauquier County, license issued 13 November 1780. Benjamin served in the Fauquier Militia during the Revolution under Capt. Blackwell, at the age of 16. He participated in the Battles of Monmouth, Germantown and Brandywine. During his second period of enlistment he raised a company of 100 men, was appointed Captain and served under General Daniel Morgan and Col. Heath in the Third Virginia Regiment. When he was 73 years of age he received a pension (No. S 4629) while living in Lincoln Co., Ky. The land owned by Benjamin before his move to Kentucky (about 1786) comprised his own share of his father's estate and also the share that would have passed to his brother, George O'Bannon. The land extended north to present Route 698 (O'Bannon's Rd.), crossing Broad Run, to the southern line of the land his father had sold to James Nelson. It contained 295 acres, more or less. It seems that Captain Benjamin O'Bannon did not move to Kentucky for some time after 1786, as later deeds do not record that he was living out of the state in 1803 and 1811. On the 12th of February 1803 he sold all of his land southeast of Broad Run, 100 acres more or less, to his nephew James O'Bannon, son of John and Lydia (Duncan) O'Bannon. (FC D.B. 15, p. 283). James O'Bannon was to receive an adjoining 283 acres in the division of the estate of his father in 1816. All of this James O'Bannon sold to Henry Glascock (great-great grandfather of John K. Gott) and moved to Shelby Co., Ky. The 100 acres originally purchased from his uncle Benjamin O'Bannon in some way became involved in a chancery suit which was not settled until June 1831, at which time he was obliged to buy it back in order to make good his sale to Glascock, dated 25 April 1820. Captain O'Bannon sold the rest of his land, or most of it, 16 Nov. 1811 to William Urton (FC D.B. 18, p. 298). This tract, containing 165½ acres, lies precisely in the center of the "Great Meadow" tract, near the Old Tavern and "home of the Gold Cup Races". It is described as "part of a larger tract whereon the said O'Bannon now lives." The fact of the matter is that, having sold the area southeast of Broad Run, only 29 acres of the "larger" tract remained. On that 29 acres stood his house, called "Pravda", and the reason that it was not sold was that it was claimed by George Chapman. That claim was voided by a resurvey of the Chapman land, conclusively demonstrating that it was on the original O'Bannon patent. "Pravda" was sold in 1823 to Jeremiah Strother by Francis O'Bannon, son of Benjamin O'Bannon. (FC D.B. 27, p. 258). The old house burned in Dec. 1958 and the lone chimney stood until recent years when Rt. 17 was widened to a four-lane road. On a site just back of the original house, Mr. Ted Berry, brother of Mrs. Lou B. O'Bannon (Mrs.. John Norris O'Bannon, Sr.) built a fine home, christened "Long view". Eleanor Ash (sometimes Helon, Elon, etc.) was a daughter of Francis Ash of Fauquier County who died in 1774, testate. (FC W.B. 1, p. 249). Eleanor also received an inheritance from her sister, Mary Ash, in 1814. (W.B. 6, p. 2). Benjamin O'Bannon died in Kentucky in 1838 and Eleanor died about 1836.

ISSUE (O'BANNON):

102. Elizabeth[4], m: Edward Bailey, 1803.
103. Ellen (or Helen)[4], m: Joseph Vaughn
104. Harriet[4], m: Frederick Shackleford, 27 Dec. 1820, Lincoln Co., Ky.
105. Dolly[4], m: David Simpson, Lincoln Co., Ky.
106. Mariah[4], m: Valentine Sublett, 1820, Lincoln Co., Ky.
107. John[4]
108. Francis[4], m: (1st) Sarah Payne, 4 Mar. 1830; m: (2nd) Catherine Pearl, 29 Apr. 1839.

109. William[4], b: 1803, Va.; m: 1821, Ky., Catherine Herring, living in Cass Co., Mo., 1870.
110. George[4], b: bef: 1790, Va.; d: bet. 1831-34. (the line of this family is given in: Bennett, M.T.: THE O'BANNON FAMILY (1960), and Bolenbaker, Jean, in O'BANNON GENEALOGIST, v. 2 no. 4, July 1980)

24. SAMUEL[3] O'BANNON (John[2], Bryan[1]) married Sarah (or Sally) _____ (whose maiden name has never been found and, of course, no marriage bond exists in Fauquier). Samuel O'Bannon had inherited about 165 acres from his father and remained on the property all his life. The site of his farm is located between Broad Run and the edge of the steeplechase course at "Great Meadow". Across from the course is a house and barn, neither of which are old enough to have been there during the ownership of Samuel O'Bannon, however, in a circle formed by the road between the present structures is the O'Bannon Cemetery. There is clear evidence of several graves — the spots are sunken and the grass is always a darker green. The only grave marked is that of Samuel's son Enoch4 who was born 1780 and died 1820, just two years before his father. On 2 Oct. 1819 Samuel O'Bannon, Sr. sold to Walter A. Smith, of "Mt. Eccentric", a small parcel of 4 acres, possibly to straighten out a line. At the settlement of Samuel's estate, his widow purchased the 159-acre farm from the Commissioners appointed in a chancery suit, "O'Bannon vs. O'Bannon", instituted in 1827 to settle the estate. (Fauq. Co. D.B. 29, p. 327 and D. B. 31, p. 350) On the same day Sally O'Bannon purchased the farm from the Commissioners, 17 Nov. 1830, she sold the tract to Walter A. Smith for $796.62 ½. With the sale of this farm the last of the original grant to Bryan[1] O'Bannon was sold out of the O'Bannon family.

ISSUE (O'BANNON):

+ 111.   Samuel[4]
+ 112.   Susanna[4]
+ 113.   Sarah[4]
+ 114.   Ellen[4]
+ 115.   Charles B.[4]
+ 116.   Betsy[4]
+ 117.   Nancy[4]
+ 118.   Craven[4]
  119.   Hannah[4], d: unmarried
+ 120.   Enoch[4], b: 1780; d: 1820.
  120a. Willis[4]

25. WILLIAM[3] O'BANNON (William[2], Bryan[1])in the records of Fauquier County William[3] is known as William O'Bannon, the Younger and William O'Bannon, Junior. Suits against William appear in the Minute Books of Fauquier County, Va. from March to June 1762. On 24 July 1762, William O'Bannon the Younger and Mary, his wife, sold to Alexander Farrow of Loudoun County a tract of 50 acres for £25 "on the Waggon Road that leads to Winchester it being part of a Greater tract given the aforesaid Wm. Obannon by his Grandfather Mr. Bryan Obannon, dec'd.." (FC D.B.

1, p. 366) The next year he sold the rest of his estate to Alexander Farrow. (D.B. 2, p. 76, 13 July 1763). This tract was clearly beyond the northermost limits of his grandfather's patent, but was south of the Grinan patent, then owned by the Scott heirs (known today as "Gordonsdale"). It was approximately at the point where the present Route 17 meets Route 245 and probably included the ground on which Lawrence's Tavern was later built. In all William sold Alexander Farrow 306 acres about 100 acres more than was given to him under his grand father's will — indicating that the heirs found the "real" corners of their Grandfather Bryan's grants.

In 1766 Farrow sold both tracts back to John O'Bannon, Sr. There is no record that Alexander Farrow ran a tavern on his property, although it was already at the junction of two roads. There was a tavern (sometimes called "ordinary") on the site in 1766, known as O'Bannon's Tavern. It appears from a law suit in Fauquier County that the tavern, or ordinary, was run by William O'Bannon, Sr., and the cast of characters includes several names already familiar. (O'Bannon vs. Rust). Sometime after this date they moved to North Carolina and a William O'Bannon was on the Tax List in Bute County, N.C. in 1771. In March 1774 William was witness to a deed from Robert Duncan to Joseph Red Dick. William O'Bannon received payments in North Carolina for service in the Revolution as a private from enlistment on 20 July 1776, for 2⅓ years, until discharged 6 Nov. 1778. (N.C. in the Revolution, p. 151) The next records of William and Mary O'Bannon are found in Laurens County, S.C. Some of the families of this couple have a tradition that this family stopped off in Kentucky on their way to Missouri. However, the source of this could find no proof. (THE O'BANNON GENEALOGIST, n.d. ca: 1981)

ISSUE (O'BANNON):

121. John[4], b: 25 Nov. 1771; d: 16 March 1838. He m: 1796, Elizabeth Polly Allen, b: 1778; d: 1853. This couple are the ancestors of the late O'Bannon genealogist, Walter O'Bannon, of Tulsa, Okla.
122. Thomas[4], b: 1768, m: Tabitha Razzon or Raggan
123. William[4], b: Jones Co., N.C.
Possibly others.

26. ELIZABETH[3] O'BANNON (William[2], Bryan[1]) married (1st) James Nelson, in Fauquier County, Va., 1 Febr. 1765. In October 1770 John O'Bannon sold 100 acres, including the 50 acres originally purchased by Farrow on which the tavern, mentioned above, presumably stood, to James Nelson, who had married Elizabeth. In the May Court 1772 Betty (Elizabeth) Nelson obtained a license to keep an ordinary at her house on the Winchester Road. We shall see more of the tavern as we proceed further into the genealogy. James Nelson died in Fauq. Co. on 14 Nov. 1771, and, according to Bradshaw (see above) "leaving a widow and two daughters". Another source says there was a son, Benjamin Nelson. His estate was inventoried by Samuel Grigsby, John Obanon and James Foley on 14 Nov. 1771 (hardly the day he died!) (FC W.B. 1, p. 188). On 15 October 1792, his administratrix, Betty Asberry, returned her account and she was found to be indebted to the estate in the amount of £116.4.7. On 23 Sept. 1793 Mrs. Elizabeth Asberry's estate account was

recorded. She reported a large number of debts collected and even a larger number of balances unpaid, amounting to £227.8.2 ½.

Shortly after Nelson's death, on 27 June 1772, Betty O'Bannon Nelson married Henry Allen. His inventory was presented to the Court for recording by his widow, Betty Allen, on 14 April 1775. His estate amounted to £29.12.3. (W.B. 1, p. 276) Henry's estate was indebted to James Nelson's estate! Evidently, Elizabeth married again, to William Asberry, but no marriage license is recorded. This was probably William Asberry, Jr. as the inventory of one William Asberry, with widow Jane, was recorded on 22 Sept. 1794. On 27 July 1792, William Asbury, of Leeds Parish, and Betty, his wife, sell to John Wake a tract of 224 acres, of which one hundred acres were in woods, located on the west side of the Pignut Ridge. This deed was recorded 23 June 1795. That same year (1795) William Asbury (or Asberry) appears on a tax list in Mason County, Kentucky. It is not known when Elizabeth (O'Bannon) Asberry died for on the marriage record of her daughter in 1796, Mason County, Ky. Marriage Records, parents are listed as William and Hannah Asberry. (THE O'BANNON GENEALOGIST — this might not be the daughter of William & Betty (O'Bannon) Asberry!) There is a will for a William Asberry (Elizabeth O'Bannon's husband ?) in Harrison Co., Ky., W.B. B, p. 203)

ISSUE (NELSON):

124.   Benjamin[4]
125.   Catherine[4]
126.   Elizabeth[4]

ISSUE (ASBERRY):

127.   Susanna[4]

27. BRYANT[3] O'BANNON (William[2], Bryan[1]) was one of the grandchildren named in the will of Bryan[1] O'Bannon in which he received a negro girl, Cate. He was born ca: 1747 and married Ruth Burgess, daughter of Francis Burgess, between March 1770 and Oct. 1771. In his will dated 26 March 1770, Francis Burgess named his daugher, Ruth Burgess; but in the settlement of his estate in Oct. 1771 his dau. Ruth's part was paid to her husband, Brian O'Bannon. (FC W.B. 2, p. 38) Bryan and Ruth O'Bannon moved to Salisbury Dist., N.C. where Bryan later fought in the Revolution. During which time, Ruth was apparently staying with her relatives in Virginia, as the 1850 Census shows that their son, Dawson Burgess O'Bannon, was born in 1780, in Virginia.

The following issue of Bryant and Ruth (Burgess) O'Bannon are taken from DeHuff, p. 52 and THE O'BANNON GENEALOGIST, v. 1, no. 4)

ISSUE (O'BANNON):

128.   Dawson Burgess[4]

129.   John[4]
130.   William[4]

28. MILDRED[3] O'BANNON (William[2], Bryan[1]) In the records of Fauquier County is a lawsuit brought in Oct. 1770 by William O'Bannon on behalf of Mildred, "an Infant under the age of twenty-one years" as her "next friend" against Samuel Rust. According to the declaration Mr. Rust proposed marriage to Mildred and under these pretenses made improper advances and "prevailed upon her to anticipate what he called his happiness and to permit him to use her as his wife from which Commerce she proved with Child." In the meantime, Mr. Rust married "with one Mary Baley — by means whereof she the s'd Plft. is greatly Injuried in marrying creditably with any other person and saith she is the worse and heath Damage to the Value of Five Hundred pounds." According to Alex'r. Farrow, a witness, this happened on the 5th or 6th January 1766 — the testimony was given on 26 Sept. 1769 before Thomas Marshall and John Moffett. The jury found in favor of the Plft. and fined Samuel Rust One Hundred Pounds Current Money. From this suit we learn that William O'Bannon, father of Mildred, kept an "ordinary" (the Old Tavern) in his home and his wife's name was Elizabeth. There were two beds in the "Publick" room of the house. One of them was occupied by John Chapman, a youth of 15 years, and William Owens, the other by Mildred O'Bannon. Alexander Farrow "lay by the fireside the said night." According to Farrow, "Elizabeth O'Bannon, mother of the said Mildred, asked Samuel Rust to go & lay down by Milley, and that the said Rust accordingly went and lay the Remainder part of the said Night." This was the same tavern, or ordinary, kept later by Mildred's sister, Elizabeth (Betty) Nelson. Samuel Rust was a son of John Rust of Westmoreland & Fauquier Counties. According to the RUST OF VIRGINIA, by E. M. Rust (1940, pp. 25 & 100), he married Mary Lee Bailey. For a while Samuel Rust lived in Fauquier, near the O'Bannons, but later moved to Kanawha County, Va. (now W. Va.) where he died and is buried near Coca, W. Va. in the Rust family cemetery. He was the father of 11 children, besides his deserted child by Mildred. One cannot help wondering what became of her ...!

29. John[3] O'BANNON (William[2], Bryan[1]) very little is known about this John O'Bannon and there being two or three makes if difficult to distinguish one from the other. The 1769 will of Simon Miller names "John O'Bannon son of William" as one of his executors. There are several other references to John O'Bannon, calling him Junior, in the Fauquier records. At the April Court 1782 we find "On the motion of John Obanon and Frances his Wife late the Widow of Nimrod Ashby, dec'd. It is ordered that Hezekiah Turner, John Thomas Chunn, and John Edmonds, Gent. or any 2 of them, do allott to the said Frances her dower in the slaves whereof Martin Ashby, son of the said Nimrod is possessed." Frances Wright, b: ca: 1742, was a dau. of Francis & Ann (_____) Wright, she married (1st) Capt. Nimrod Ashby who d: 29 June 1764, killed by the Delaware Indians at Hanging Rock. They had two sons: Martin and Thomas Bryan Ashby. It is not known whether John and Frances (Wright) (Ashby) O'Bannon had any children.

29a. CATHERINE[3] O'BANNON (William[2], Bryan[1]) m: Joseph Duncan, Jr. He was the son of Joseph & Lydia Duncan. Joseph and Catherine (O'Bannon) Duncan removed to Harrison County, Ky. where he died, testate, 1822. Catherine was b: ca: 1748 and died before 1810; Joseph was born 1742 and died in Harrison Co., Ky. They were married before 1764 when "William Obanion of parish of Hamilton, planter and Elizabeth, his wife," gave to Joseph Duncan, Jun'r .. "in consideration of the Natural love and affection which we have and do bear unto the said Joseph Duncan .. 50 acres .. being part of a greater tract on which the said Obanion now lives .." The deed was recorded 27 Sept. 1764 in D.B. 2, p. 195. The descendants claim that since the deed does not state the relationship to the grantors, it was Catherine, their daughter and Joseph, their son-in-law they were giving the land to and not the son of Elizabeth O'Bannon by a previous marriage.

30. ELIZABETH[3] MILLER (Mary Anne[2], Bryan[1]) married Elias Edmonds I, b: 1726; d: 1784, about 1750. He was an officer in Braddock's Army and also was a magistrate in Fauquier County. They were both buried on the old Edmonds home place near Warrenton.

ISSUE (EDMONDS):

131. Judith[4], b: ca: 1751, m. Richard Buckner, 27 Feb. 1772.
132. Anne[4], b: ca: 1753, m: Ephriam Hubbard, 27 Dec. 1774.
133. Elizabeth (Betty)[4], b: ca: 1755, m: Peter Bruin, 27 Feb. 1781.
134. Elias[4], b: ca: 1757; d: 1800; m. Frances Edmonds, 11 Jan. 1786, his cousin.

FOURTH GENERATION

44. JOSEPH⁴ O'BANNON (John³, John², Bryan¹) married (1ˢᵗ) Elizabeth (Bullitt) Grigsby, widow of William Grigsby and m: (2ⁿᵈ) Elizabeth Marrs Lewis, dau. of William and Ann (Montgomery) Lewis of "Mt. Pleasant", Fauquier County. Francis Montgomery of "Rose Mount", Prince William Co, Va. was her uncle. Major Joseph O'Bannon amassed a large estate during his lifetime, including a portion of the Carr-Tebbs estate called "White Plains", from which the town of The Plains got its name. Major O'Bannon's estate encompassed most of the present town. After his death, in 1824, his estate was sold (after giving his widow her one-third portion) to Thomas Foster, the first of that family in the area. Elizabeth (Lewis) O'Bannon, m: (2ⁿᵈ), 17 Oct. 1826, Peter Pierce. He (Peter Pierce) m: (2ⁿᵈ), 17 Sept. 1834, Eliza J. M. Wither, widow of Daniel Withers who had been a Clerk of the Fauquier County Court. The Pierce family was connected with the Hume and McGeorge families of Fauquier. The O'Bannon family cemetery was reserved in the transfer of the property, and unless it was incorporated into the Foster cemetery at "Whitewood", it has disappeared. A lengthy chancery suit, entitled, "Waters vs. Lewis", in Fauquier County, to settle Joseph's estate ensued. Henry Marrs Lewis, Elizabeth's brother, was the executor of the estate.

ISSUE (O'BANNON) - First marriage:

+ 135.   Parmenas Bullitt⁵
  136.   Lydia⁵, m: John Fishback, son of Josiah. Had: 1) Elizabeth, m: in Ky. 2) Ann, m: Fenton Owens and 3) Louisa, n. m.

ISSUE (O'BANNON) - Second Marriage:

  137.   Nancy Marrs⁵, m: 1 Oct. 1832, Thomas S. Waters, M.D.
  138.   Elvira Elizabeth⁵, m: 13 Dec. 1832, Elijah J. Strother
  139.   Joseph O'Rear⁵
  140.   Aramanta Catharine⁵, d: yg., 20 Oct. 1832
  141.   William Searles⁵, to Missouri; Richard Strother, guardian
  142.   James Henry⁵, d: yg., 21 July 1830

45. ELIZABETH⁴ O'BANNON (John³, John², Bryan¹) married (1ˢᵗ) Enoch Smith, d: 1803; m. (2ⁿᵈ), Francis Triplett, 20 Nov. 1812, Fauquier County. "Marriage agreement of Elizabeth Smith of Fauquier County and Francis Triplett of Loudoun County. The marriage of Francis Triplett and Elizabeth, relict of Enoch Smith, shortly to be solemnized. Francis Triplett and his heirs promise "not to meddle with take, claim or dispose of any part of the estate of Elizabeth Smith." She m: (3ʳᵈ), William Grigsby, 22 May 1826, Fauquier County.

ISSUE (SMITH):

  143.   John⁵
  144.   Elijah⁵
  145.   Hedgman⁵   the last 3 inherited land on Watery Mt.

146. Isham[5], m: Margaret Ayres, dau. of Charles, 28 Oct. 1816.
147. Elias[5]
148. Lucinda[5], m: Enoch D. Withers, 13 Feb. 1809.
149. Enoch D.[5] (probably the child born after father's death mentioned in will (W.B. 3, p. 437). Enoch D. Smith died in 1828 (W.B. 10, p. 386). He left his mother, Elizabeth Grigsby, all land, his brother, Hedgman Smith, the land after his mother's death. And to his stepfather, William Grigsby, 3 ¼ yards of shepherds extra superfine blue cloth — to him and his heirs forever!

46. JAMES[4] O'BANNON (John[3], John[2], Bryan[1]) married Lucy N. O'Bannon, dau. of Thomas and Hannah (Barker) O'Bannon, q.v., 10 March 1802. Lucy was b: 1784 and died 1874. They lived in Henry County, Kentucky. James O'Bannon had inherited the farm now known as "Chetwood" (built by the Skinker family) now owned by Vincent Sheehy. On this property, near the base of the Pignut Mt. is the old O'Bannon home and cemetery. On 18 June 1831, after a lawsuit involving the property, he and his wife, Lucy, of Shelby Co., Ky. deeded the property to Henry Glascock (great-great grandfather of the compiler). Henry Glascock and his wife, Jane Linton (Combs) Glascock are buried in the O'Bannon Cemetery near the old house. Only one tombstone survives — William K. Skinker used the enclosed cemetery for a hog pen!   (F.C. D.B. 31, p. 418 and D.B. 36, p. 2)

ISSUE (O'BANNON):

150. Frances Ann[5]
151. Alcy Duncan[5]
152. Elizabeth Hannah[5]
153. John[5]
154. James[5]
155. Tom[5]
156. Lucy Neville[5]
157. Mary Jane[5]

47. JEMIMA[4] O'BANNON (John[3], John[2], Bryan[1]) m: 30 Nov. 1786, Archibald Johnston.

48. ISHAM[4] O'BANNON (John[3], John[2], Bryan[1]), b: 9 April 1769; d: 1 March 1845. On 23 Nov. 1798 license were issued to Capt. Isham O'Bannon and Polly [Mary] Winn, daughter of Minor Winn of "Rock Hill", near The Plains. Walter O'Bannon had in his records that Capt. O'Bannon had married, first, Mildred Roberts — he must have confused this with Isham's nephew, Parmenis B. O'Bannon's second wife. Mildred Ames noted that there was another license issued to one Isham O'Bannon and Cathrine O'Bannon, 25 Aug. 1814, Enoch O'Bannon, bondsman. Someone wrote to her, in THE O'BANNON GENEALOGIST, that the two Ishams were not the same. In another instance, Ms. Ames stated that Catherine O'Bannon was the daugher of Samuel[3] (John[2]), however,

no Catherine O'Bannon, nor an Isham, is listed in the settlement of Samuel's estate in the late 1820's. The latest genealogy on the family of Capt. Isham O'Bannon does not mention that he ever married again after the death of Polly (Winn) O'Bannon. (Charles W. Jenkins: THE O'BANNON FAMILY OF FAUQUIER COUNTY, VIRGINIA, JEFFERSON COUNTY, KENTUCKY, MONTGOMERY COUNTY, ILLINOIS). Mr. Jenkins states that, "Isham, taking his son Richard with him went to Kentucky in 1816 to claim his share of the land he had been bequeathed by his father, John, Jr." He settled "about 8 miles East of Louisville." On 1 Nov. 1817, Capt. O'Bannon gave his power of attorney to his brother, Major Joseph O'Bannon, as guardian of his (Isham's) children: Susanna, Mary S., Narcissa G. and Minor W. O'Bannon, "to receive from the exors. of Minor Winn any property, etc. which might be due him from Winn's estate."

ISSUE (O'BANNON)

158. Ambrose[5], m: (1) Elizabeth Bashaw, d: 8 May 1847, aged 37 years; m: (2) Emily (Durham) Morehead.
159. Armistead[5]
160. Isham Bushrod[5], b: 1812, m: Mary Margaret Smith (not mentioned in guardian bond of Isham O'Bannon in Fauq. Co. for his minor children?)
161. James[5]
162. Richard Winn[5], b: 1808; d: 1883, M: Matilda Dorsey, 1830, Ky. (see: Jenkins, ibid.)
163. Minor Winn[5], m: (1) Jane Richardson; m: (2) Julia Barnet; m: (3) Mrs. Elizabeth (Harrison) Payne
164. Narcissa G.[5]
165. Susannah[5], m: Levin Lawrence Dorsey
166. Eliza[5]
167. Jane[5]
168. Mary S.[5]

49. ELIAS[4] O'BANNON (John[3], John[2]) married Elizabeth Grigsby, 24 July 1799, Fauquier Co., Va., Joseph O'Bannon, bondsman. He was born in Oct. 1771 and d: 3 July 1828 and is buried on the Hardesty Farm, near Eminence, Henry Co., Ky. In 1809 Elias O'Bannon was living in Prince William County, where he was doing business with, or for, Francis Montgomery. (FC, D.B. 17, p. 421) On 3 Nov. 1810, he and his wife, Elizabeth, of Pr. Wm. Co. joined other heirs of William Grigsby in selling land on head branches of Aquia Run in the County of Fauquier and Stafford. (FC, D.B. 18, p. 714).

50. JOHN A. O'BANNON (John[3], John[2], Bryan[1]) married Frances (called Fanny) O'Bannon, b: 1787; d: 4 April 1840, license issued 20 December 1808, Fauquier County. Thomas O'Bannon gave his consent and James O'Bannon was bondsman. Fanny was the daughter of Thomas and Hannah (Barker) O'Bannon (#76). Thomas O'Bannon, the son of William and Anne (Neville) O'Bannon, lived near his father at Marshall, Va. The old Thomas O'Bannon home, probably built by a former owner, John Proudfoot, is still standing, formerly owned by W. D. Stephenson, and now George R.

Thompson, III. On the farm is the O'Bannon Cemetery, where Fanny is buried, probably John and others of Thomas' family. John died before March 1811 when Fanny received his portion of his father's estate. John O'Bannon, Jr.'s estate was appraised on the 8 Febr. 1811 (FC W.B. 5, p. 211). Fanny received 283 acres in the division of the estate of John[3] O'Bannon, Sr. on 11 October 1816 (FC W.B. 6, p. 277) — this was located near the Pignut Mt. Frances O'Bannon's will was proved 25 May 1840, in which she left the bulk of her estate to her grandchildren, the children of her only daughter, Jane H. (O'Bannon) Welch, first wife of Sylvester Welch, Jr. According to the descendants, the Combs family, the grandchildren never received their full share of their grandmother's estate. By the time they were grown Sylvester Welch, Jr. had incorporated their estate into his own, which he squandered. A son by the second marriage of Mr. Welch stepped in and saved what was left of the estate, shortly after the Civil War, forcing his father to turn over his affairs to him. The same Combs heirs insist that the Welch-Murray fortune had its basis with the fortune left by John and Fanny O'Bannon. Fanny O'Bannon acquired several lots and houses in the town of Salem (now Marshall) which descended to the grandchildren.

ISSUE (O'BANNON):

+ 169.   Jane H.[5], d: 14 July 1833, aged 24 years. (Tombstone on Flint Hill Farm, near Marshall, Va.)

51. WILLIAM[4] O'BANNON (James[3], John[2], Bryan[1]) married, 14 Jan. 1800, Ann D. Smith (sometimes called Nancy), dau. of William and Elizabeth (Doniphan) Smith of "Mt. Eccentric," Fauquier County. William O'Bannon had inherited 283 acres on the Pignut Mt. from his father, which was near "Mt. Eccentric". (W.B. 6, p. 277). There is a sketch of William Smith in that genealogy, which should have been outlawed, by Lucy Montgomery Smith Price: THE SYDNEY-SMITH AND CLAGETT-PRICE GENEALOGY, (1927), p. 53. On 28 June 1804, William O'Bannon and Nancy, his wife, sold to her brother, Walter A. Smith, for £500, her 1/7th portion of all lands in Fauquier County which had descended to her from her father. William O'Bannon sold to James Morrison, 15 Oct. 1816, 565 acres (his inheritance and another tract not accounted for) on the Pignut Ridge and on the waters of Broad Run. The land straddled the Ridge on the east and west, with corners to John Tomlin, Skinker and the lands of John O'Bannon, Jur., dec'd. and William O'Bannon.

59. SARAH[4] FOLEY (Sarah[3], John[2], Bryan[1]) License were issued to Francis Watts and Sarah Foley, in Fauquier Co., on 16 Oct. 1777, James Foley, bondsman. On 23 Oct. 1786, they received a lease from the agent of George William Fairfax, George Nicholas, for 188 acres, called Lot No. 14, on the Rappahannock Mountain, near the Old Tavern. The lease for "three lives" was made out to Francis Watts, Sarah, his wife and their daughter, Suckey. One year later, Andrew O'Bannon, Sarah's uncle, received a similar lease to "Lot No. 16" for 150 acres. The conditions of both leases were the same: within 3 years they had to build a good dwelling house at least 20 feet by 16 feet and a barn 20 feet square. They were also required to set out 200 winter apple trees and 200 peach trees. The Colvert family, whom we shall meet shortly, also lived on the mountain.

The date of Watts' death is not certain, however, there is an inventory of his estate in Fauquier, dated 19 Oct. 1787. Sarah and her two daughters, Edie and Susannah ("Sukey") continued to live on the lease. Susannah married Jeremiah Strother and his mother-in-law, Sarah (Foley) Watts, assigned to him "all my right & title of the within lease." This is all that is recorded — the descendants of Jeremiah and Susannah (Watts) Strother still own the original lease. Sarah (Foley) Watts died in September 1807 but her daughter, Sukey Strother, lived until 1855. (FC W. B. 4, p. 406) She left a considerable estate and to read the inventory would make an antique lover envious.

ISSUE (WATTS):

170.   Edy[5] (or Edith), m: 6 Dec. 1801, Hezekiah Cockrell
+ 171.   Susannah[5]

72. WILLIAM[4] O'BANNON (William[3], John[2]) married, (1st), 1796, Peggy Francisco and (2nd) 1809, Eliza Wilson. He died 19 March 1857 in Breckinridge Co., Ky. He was in Woodford Co., Ky. in 1819 when he gave his power of attorney to George F. Cotton to attend to his portion of his father's estate in Fauquier. (FC D.B. 17, p. 660)

ISSUE (O'BANNON)   (1st marriage):

172.   George Francisco[5], b: 1800; d: 1885, Illinois
173.   Nancy[5], m: Henry Lewis Miller, Tuscumbia, Ala.
174.   Margaret[5], m: 1820, Samuel M. Perry, Lawrence Co., Ala.

ISSUE 2nd Marriage:

175.   Henry W.[5]
175a.   Elijah P.[5]
175b.   Caroline[5]
175c.   John Russell[5]
175d.   Joseph[5]
175e.   Presley Neville[5], b: 1824, Ky.; d: 1881, Harrison Co., Ind.

73. PRESLEY NEVILLE[4] O'BANNON (William[3]) was born near Marshall, Fauquier Co., Va., 1776. As a young man he served as Deputy Sheriff of Fauquier County. He enlisted and was commissioned Lieutenant in the U. S. Marine Corps. The expedition across the North African desert from Egypt to the city of Derna in Tripoli in 1805 is well-known. Lt. O'Bannon led the assault force, rushed to the base of the flag pole, lowered the Tripolian flag and ran up the Flag of the United States — the first time over a captured fortress in the Old World. He returned home a hero and years later the Commonwealth of Virginia presented him with a handsome sword — now the proud possession of the Marine Corps. He returned home just months before the death of his father in October, 1807. He attended the January 1807 Court of Fauquier County, where

not a word of his heroism is mentioned; he had other business. It was ordered "that the Overseers of the Poor bind Hammett Cairo to Presley N. O'Bannon." Just exactly what that meant is questionable — did he adopt a native of North Africa, possibly an Egyptian? (FC Min. Book 1806-1809, Jan. Court, 1807) On 24 Jan. 1809, in Frederick Co., Va. he married Matilda Heard, grand-daughter of the renown General Daniel Morgan.

It must have been shortly after their marriage that the couple moved to Russellville, Logan Co., Ky. He served for a number of years in the Kentucky legislature and having become a Mason in New York, probably during his stay in that city awaiting transportation to the Mediterrean, he affliliated with the Russellville Masonic Lodge. It is said by several sources that the couple had children — one source reports that he returned from North Africa to find his son dead, which is impossible, since he was not married when he left the United States. Another says that he had a son, Eaton, named for the civilian "General" William Eaton, whose idea it was to invade Tripoli. Another, that they had a daughter named Elizabeth. Matilda seems to have had mental problems — acute enough to have her committed to the state institution for the insane where she died. He went to Henry County to live with relatives, where he died, 12 Sept. 1850. His tombstone, decorated with an American eagle and cannon, states that he was "aged 74 years". In 1920 his remains were removed to Frankfort, Ky. There have been three U. S. naval vessels named for him — the last was commissioned 15 Dec. 1979 at Pascagoula, Mississippi. Attending the commissioning was Lt. Cmdr. Kenneth O'Bannon, a descendant of Samuel O'Bannon of Fauquier County, thro' his son Enoch. Lt. Cmdr. O'Bannon's father is Paul O'Bannon, son of the late James Keith O'Bannon. The first O'BANNON, a destroyer, was launched 28 Febr. 1919 under the sponsorship of Mrs. Henry O'Bannon Cooper, wife of the great-great nephew of Lt. O'Bannon, thro' his brother Bryant of Rappahannock County.

On 23 June 1818, Presley N. O'Bannon & Matilda, his wife, of Kentucky, sold to Thomas O'Bannon for $800 the land he inherited from his father, described as "a certain tract of land situate in the said county of Fauquier joining the land taken up by Capt. Skinker, now belonging to William Skinker under the Pignut Ridge on the south side, which tract of land was granted by the Proprietor of the Northern Neck .. to John O'Bannon by Patent .. 14 July 1742 and said to contain 189 acres .. and by the said John O'Bannon was devised to William O'Bannon under whose will it was allotted to the said Presley N. O'Bannon and the said Thomas O'Bannon .."

75. ALEXANDER[4] O'BANNON (William[3], John[2]) was issued a license to marry Sally McClanaham, 14 April 1825, Presley N. O. Lawrence, bondsman. In 1813 he was allotted a tract adjoining Daniel Flowerree's land (Lot #8), of his father's estate. He received no portion of his mother's dower — his equal share was to be paid to him in clothing. There is no record of the disposition of his land, or a record of Alexander in Fauquier County.

76. THOMAS[4] O'BANNON (William[3]) married Hannah Barker, 21 Jan. 1783, Fauquier Co., Va., a dau. of William Barker who came to America from Wales according to a sketch of the family by Mrs. John L. Cleaver. On 13 July 1799 he purchased from John Monroe Lot No. 23 in Salem

(Marshall) and the log house he built on the lot was burned within 10 years ago as a fire drill! In 1816 the tax records show that he also owned Lot No. 20. In 1801 John Proudfoot assigned to Thomas O'Bannon his lease in the Manor of Leeds which joined the back lines of the town of Salem on the south. This farm he purchased from the Marshall family and descended to his son, Presley N. O'Bannon, and was known as "Flint Hill Farm," now owned by George R. Thompson, III. The O'Bannon home still stands — in ruins.

In Fauq. Co. Minute Book 1832-33, pp. 131-132 we find the declaration of Thomas O'Bannon for a pension for service in the American Revolution. He made the declaration on 31 Aug. 1832 when he was 76 years of age. He states: "I entered the service of the United States on the 4th of Sept. 1780 under the command of Capt. James Winn, I was drafted to go to the South, I marched from the county of Fauquier and South of Virginia to Hilsborough in the state of N. C., General Smallwood commanded us for a short time then I was put under the command of Gen. Morgan who commanded us to the time we were dismissed. I was at the taking of Rudgely fort I should have been at the battle of Cowpens but I was sent near the British lines to collect the sick and bring them to Salsbury and while on that business the battle was fought. And at that time I received a letter from General Morgan commanding me to march towards Virginia with the sick. I was the quarter master sergeant though the campaign. I was discharged the last day of February 1781, the draft being for six months." Thomas O'Bannon stated that he was born in Fauquier County in 1757. He died some time before June 1834 when an inventory of his estate was recorded in Fauquier County.

ISSUE (O'BANNON):

176. Lucy Neville[5], b: 1 Feb. 1784; d: 15 Sept. 1874, m: 10 March 1802, James O'Bannon (see #46)
177. William[5], b: 1 Feb. 1784; m: Ann Eliza _____. Had: 1) Mary Ann[6] (probably more)
178. Susan[5], m: William Streit (or Stright), 18 April 1817
+ 179. Presley Neville[5]
180. Armistead[5], n.m.
181. Nancy (or Ann)[5], m: William McIntyre, 14 April 1810, Fauquier Co. Had: 1) Ann, m: Wm. Shields, a merchant in Salem (Marshall), 1831.
182. Frances[5] (or Fanny), b: 1787; d: 4 April 1840, buried at "Flint Hill Farm", m: John O'Bannon (see #50)

77. JOSEPH[4] O'BANNON (William[3], John[2], Bryan[1])b: 1758; d: 1824; m: 1779, Martha Weldon, who died March 1826. On 1 March 1815, Joseph sold his inheritance, Lot No. 2, allotted to him. At the time he was living in Hardy County, Va. (now W. Va.)

ISSUE (O'BANNON):

183. Elizabeth Ann[5]
184. Joseph P. H.[5]

185. Judge William[5]
186. Mary[5]
187. Welton[5]
188. John[5]

78. AGNES (or Aggatha)[4] O'BANNON (William[3], John[2]) married 13 April 1801, George Jeffries. He enlisted at Salem, in 1814 and served as a Private and Corporal in Col. Renoe's Regt. of the Virginia Militia until he died in camp 18 Nov. 1814. She was allowed a pension on account of his service in 1853, aged seventy-five years. At the time of his death, George Jeffries was camped near Ellicott's Mills, Md. On 27 Dec. 1819, Agatha Jeffries was appointed Guardian for her children in the amount of $4,000. She had inherited a nice farm from her father which she farmed.

ISSUE (JEFFRIES):

189. Addison[5], b: 14 Jan. 1802; d: 3 Aug. 1835, m: 1831, Angelina W. Jett, dau. of George W. Jett and Nancy Wickcliffe (DAR, Vol. 1055, No. 211,521)
190. Nancy[5], m: 28 May 1824, Fauq. Co., Alex. W. Lawrence.
+ 191. Presley Neville[5], b: 17 Nov. 1805; d: 28 Dec. 1887; M: Nancy Utterback, dau. of William, 30 April 1827.
192. Sally[5]
+ 193. Drusilla[5], b: 5 Aug. 1811; d: 23 Sept. 1876.

79. MARY (or POLLY)[4] O'BANNON (William[3]) married William Utterback, 4 July 1799, Fauquier County, Va.

ISSUE (UTTERBACK):

194. Emily[5], b: 11 May 1800, m: John McClanahan
195. Bryant O.[5], b: 1812; d: 1898, m: 23 May 1861, Susan Glascock.
196. Nancy[5], m: Presley N. Jeffries (see #191)
197. Joseph[5]
198. William[5]
199. Wilfred N.[5] m: 1st, Drusilla Jeffries (see #193)
200. Elizabeth[5], m: Wm. D. Lawrence.

80. SALLY[4] O'BANNON (sometimes referred to as Elizabeth) (William[3]) married 9 February 1794, Elijah Pepper, son of Samuel and Elizabeth (Holton) Pepper, b: 1767 and d: in Woodford Co., Ky. in 1831. Sally (or Sarah) O'Bannon was b: in Fauquier Co. (near Marshall) 17 Sept. 1770 and d: in Ky., 26 August 1848. The Pepper family owned a portion of the Rev. Alexander Scott's grant, near the present town of Marshall, adjoining William O'Bannon. The grant was known as "Stony Spring" — a portion of which, "Meadow Grove", is still owned by Scott descendants (1991). Shortly

after their marriage, Elijah and Sarah Neville (O'Bannon) Pepper migrated to Kentucky, with Sally's brother, John O'Bannon. John O'B. had done extensive surveying in Ohio and Kentucky prior to moving there permanently. Elijah Pepper and John O'Bannon built a distillery just below the big spring that gushes from a cave back of the court house at Versailles, Woodford County, Ky., in which they distilled whiskey in a limited way. The partnership continued for several years, or until Elijah Pepper bought a large tract of land seven miles below the spring on Glenn's Creek, when the partnership was dissolved. John O'Bannon continued the distillation of whiskey at Versailles. Elijah Pepper erected on his farm a comfortable log house on an elevated slope above the creek that faces the Versailles and Millville road, and in the creek below he erected a distillery plant where he continued to manufacture "Old Pepper". On his farm he raised the grain that entered into the manufacture of his liquid product. After the death of Elijah, his son Oscar Pepper took charge and continued the business of his father until about 1865. In the meantime, the brands of "Old Pepper" and "Old Crow" had grown very popular, due largely to the fact that the elder Pepper had kept in his employ a highly educated Scotsman, a trained chemist, who was the distiller. The name of this Scotsman was James Crow, and the famous brands that he distilled made a fortune for the Peppers. The descendants of Elijah Pepper continued in the whiskey making business, which "culminated in the death of John Barleycorn in the year of our Lord, 1920." (Copied from an unidentified source in compiler's notes.)

ISSUE (PEPPER):

201. Elijah Enoch[5]
202. William O'Bannon[5]
203. Elizabeth H.[5], m: Dr. John Sullinger, Woodford Co., Ky. 4 August 1818.
204. Samuel[5], m: Mahala Perry
205. Nancy[5]
206. Presley[5], m: Eleanor Wallace
207. Amanda[5]
208. Matilda[5], m: Samuel Perry, 2 May 1824, Woodford County.
209. Oscar[5], m: Nannie Edwards

81. NANCY[4] O'BANNON (William[3], John[2], Bryan[1]) married Mason Lawrence, 24 March 1788. He died 1836. Mason Lawrence had succeeded to the ownership of "Lawrence's Old Tavern" from the O'Bannon family and probably lived there until Nancy inherited the home of her father. The farm and site of the home has since been known locally as the "Lawrence Place" about a mile from the present town of Marshall (formerly called Salem) Fauquier County. The O'Bannon cemetery is located about 100 yards from the site of the old house and until recently was maintained by the descendants of the Lawrence and Utterback families. After the death of Mrs. Drucilla Smith (Utterback) Russell the farm was sold, leaving the family for the first time since the 18th century when William O'Bannon purchased the place.

ISSUE (LAWRENCE):

210. William M.[5], m: (1st) Sally S. Jeffries, 13 Feb. 1839 m: (2nd) Mary M. Priest, 23 May 1844.
211. Alexander W.[5], m: Nancy Jeffries, 28 May 1824.
212. Nancy[5], m: Willis Priest, 18 Aug. 1818.
213. Presley Neville[5]
214. Agatha[5]
215. Elizabeth[5], m: John Strother, 24 Dec. 1838 — his 2nd wife.
216. John O.[5], m: (1st) Polly Larrance [sic], dau. of John, 21 Jan. 1817; m: (2nd) Mrs. Sarah Bruce (nee Sarah J. Newhouse, dau. of Ziba Newhouse) 25 Oct. 1841. John O. Lawrence d: 1844.
217. Susan M.[5], m: Isham White, 24 March 1834. They lived near Flint Hill, Va.

82. BRYANT[4] O'BANNON (William[3], John[2], Bryan[1]) married in Fauquier County, 8 August 1798, Polly Morris, dau. of Ann Morris. They moved to Culpeper County, that section which in 1833 became Rappahannock County. He acquired a large estate on the Rush and Thornton Rivers at Rock Mills (near Sperryville, Va.) He died 14 Dec. 1845, possessed of 900 acres of land. His will, dated 23 Oct. 1841, was proved on 14 Jan. 1846. He left to his wife Mary (Polly) ⅓[rd] of his estate, both real and personal, for her lifetime. After her death it was to be divided equally "amongst all my children." The executors (sons, John M. and Walter O'Bannon) were to sell his land in Fauquier — which he had inherited from his father. According to the Executors' account, Elder Thomas Buck, a well-known Primitive Baptist minister from Warren County preached his funeral, for which he received $5. On 30 July 1846 the Sheriff of Fauquier Co. was paid the land tax of $5.01 and one Maddux was paid $1.50 "for spirits used at sale of Fauquier land devised to be sold." No doubt, this enlivened the auction. The land was sold to his son, Joseph O'Bannon and Sylvester Welch, which Welch had paid off by Oct. 1847. In February the Executors brought a friendly suit in Rappahannock County to settle the estate, which continued on from 1846 to 1850 (probably Mary (Polly) had died by this time) ("O'Bannon vs. O'Bannon", Chancery Suit No. 103).

ISSUE (O'BANNON):

+ 218. James M.[5]
+ 219. John Maurice[5]
+ 220. Walter C.[5]
+ 221. Joseph(us) C.[5]
+ 222. Ann (Nancy)[5]
223. Sarah[5], m: 1873, James Franklin Green
+ 224. Mary A.[5], m: 1853, Elder John H. Menefee
+ 225. Charles Bryant[5]
226. Eliza[5], m: Giles A. Briggs
227. Lucy Margaret[5], m: 1852, Henry T. Sparks of Madison County, Va.
227a. Jane E.[5], m: Benjamin C. Robinson, 12 Jan. 1848, Rev. Barnett Grimsley, minister, Rappahannock Co., Va.

83. JOYCE[4] O'BANNON (William[3]) Married 13 March 1786, John Lawrence. By 1813, when the division of William O'Bannon's estate was made (F.C. W. B. 6, p. 309), Joyce Lawrence was dead and her children received Lot. No. 6, 62 ½ acres.

ISSUE: (LAWRENCE):

228.   Thomas[5]
229.   Mary (Polly)[5]
230.   Agatha[5]
231.   Catharine[5]
232.   Peter[5]
233.   John[5]
234.   Sally[5]
235.   Mason[5]

83a. JOHN[4] O'BANNON (William[3], John[2], Bryan[1]) married Mary Ann Winn in 1784. In Wm. E. Railey's "History of Woodford County, Kentucky", there are numerous references to Major John O'Bannon and the Pepper family. On p. 305 there is the following: "Major John O'Bannon was a pioneer of the county of Woodford. In 1810 his children were all married, and only he and his second wife were living in the home. They had 17 Negroes. In 1805 he was sheriff of Woodford County, and George T. Cotton, his son-in-law, was his deputy." Major John O'Bannon, in the spring of 1787 and Arthur Fox, enterprising surveyors from Ky., explored the military lands between the Little Miami and Scioto Rivers in Brown Co., Ohio. Their object was to obtain a knowledge of the region for the purpose of making choice locations of warrants as soon as the office for entries was opened. It was probably from his exploration that O'Bannon Creek received its name. A white-oak tree at the mouth of this creek was marked "O'B. Cr." as early as 1787. John O'Bannon was the first to make a survey within the present limits of Brown Co., Ohio. The first survey in the whole district is said to be that on which the town of Neville, [probably named for his mother] in Clermont County, and on the Ohio, is now situated, which was surveyed by O'Bannon, 13 November 1787. He made many surveys for Virginians entitled to military lands in this district. One of the first he entered was that for Philip Slaughter. (History of Brown County, Ohio. Beers, 1883, p. 241) Railey says that he came to Kentucky, with his brother-in-law Elijah Pepper (q.v.) in 1790. In 1795 Major O'Bannon was one of three trustees named for the town of Versailles, Ky. That Major O'Bannon was dead by 1816 is evidenced by the following deed in Fauquier County, Va. On 5 November 1816, Elijah Pepper and Sally, his wife, gave their power of attorney to George T. Cotton, only acting Exor. of John O'Bannon, dec'd, late of Woodford Co., Ky. all of the said county and state, sold to William H. Hampton, of Fauquier, stating, "whereas William O'Bannon, dec'd .. of Fauquier Co. did by his last will and testament, devise to John O'Bannon and Sally Pepper a certain tract in Fauquier in fee simple .. sd. John O'Bannon having departed this life without conveying & sd. exor. being vested with full power by the Will of said dec'd. to carry into effect the contracts of his Testator .. $1000 .. the 1st. Lott .. bounded: .. corner to Utterback & Rector .. 66 acres." (D.B. 21, p. 199, recorded: 28 May 1817).

ISSUE (O'BANNON):

236. Elizabeth[5], m: George Taylor Cotton, son of William and Frances (Taylor) Cotton, of Woodford Co., formerly of Loudoun Co., VA. They were the parents of 10 children. Railey (p. 305): Elizabeth O'Bannon, the first wife of George T. Cotton, Sr., was a daughter of Major John O'Bannon, who was a comrade-in-arms and a personal friend of General Lafayette, and when that distinguished veteran visited in Kentucky in 1825, he was entertained at "Sugar Grove", the home of Elizabeth O'Bannon Cotton, in the suburbs of Versailles."

237. Eliza[5], m: Buckam

111. SAMUEL[4] O'BANNON (Samuel[3], John[2], Bryan[1]) married Frances _____. Samuel lived in Fairfax and Loudoun Counties, VA. In 1820 and 1822 he acquired property in Loudoun County from Joseph B. Martian (Loud. Co. D.B. 3-A, p. 277 and D.B. 3-E, p. 308) At the April 1823 Court of Loudoun County he was appointed overseer of the "road commonly called the Old Leesburg road, leading from Broad Run to the Fairfax County line, being the same road whereon Joseph Meshow was overseer. James Lewis, Gent. to allot the hands to work thereon." On 8 Dec. 1830 he gave a deed of trust on the above land. He died 2 Feb. 1852 at the Loudoun Poor Farm, aged 70 years. There are no further records.

112. SUSANNA[4] O'BANNON (Samuel[3]) married 22 Oct. 1790, Martin Covert (sometimes the name is spelled Colvert) in Fauquier County. About this time there were other Coverts living near the O'Bannon family, on the Rappahannock Mt. Range, where they had leases from George Wm. Fairfax. Early in the 19th century at least one of the name, Asa Colvert, had moved to Palmyra, Missouri. One of Martin and Susanna's daughters, not named, had married one Alfred B. Owens by 1827. Mr. Owens, of Lewis County, KY. had the power of attorney of the Coverts of the same county to receive Susannah's share of Samuel's estate.

113. SARAH[4] O'BANNON (Samuel[3], John[2]) In 1829 she gave her receipt to Willis O'Bannon, Administrator of their father's estate, for her share in the estate and also for her share in the portion of her deceased sister, Hannah.

114. ELLEN[4] O'BANNON (Samuel[3]) "Helon" O'Bannon and Thomas W. Forrest assigned to Edward Shacklett their claim on the estate of Samuel O'Bannon and that of "his daughter, Hannah O'Bannon, dec'd." Thomas W. Forrest had married Nancy A. O'Bannon on 10 Feb. 1823, however there is no receipt signed by Nancy O'B. Forrest.

115. CHARLES B.[4] O'BANNON (Samuel[3]) On 16 Nov. 1822, the Merchon family conveyed to Charles B. O'Bannon, of Fauquier Co., 185 acres of land in Loudoun and Fairfax Counties, near Little River Turnpike. From the description this must have been in the vicinity of present-day Chantilly. (Loud. Co. D. B. 3-F, p. 467) According to the 1850 Census of Loudoun County, Charles B. O'Bannon, aged 65, with wife, Rosanna. He died 5 March 1854, "aged 65 years", the information being given by his son, Henry J. O'Bannon. (Loud. Co. Death Records) On 5 Feb. 1861, Harriet Lee of Fairfax Co. conveyed to Rosa O'Bannon, of Loud. Co., "the tract of Land lying in the lower part of Loudoun County .. on which the late Charles B. O'Bannon resided at the time of his death & which was sold by the late Cuthbert Powell, a Sheriff of Loudoun Co. .." (D.B. 6-E, p. 135)

The O'Bannon farm is again mentioned in 1870 and 1873 when Alonzo M. O'Bannon put in trust his 1/5th interest and Lemuel B. O'Bannon sold his 1/5th interest in 180 acres to Alonzo "formerly belonging to Rosanna O'Bannon (his mother).." (Loud. Co., D.B. 6-B, p. 60 and D.B. 6-E, p. 136).

ISSUE (O'BANNON):

238. Sophenia[5], age 28, 1850.
239. Isabella[5] age 24, 1850.
240. Alonzo M.[5], age 24, 1850.
241. Dagobet[5], age 21, 1850.
242. Henry J.[5], age 18, 1850. Died 1920, testate, Loudoun Co. VA. He left his estate to a friend and niece, Jane Fannie Peake, wife of Milton Peake of Alexandria, VA.
243. Lemuel B.[5]

116. ELIZABETH (or BETSY)[4] O'BANNON (Samuel[3], John[2], Bryan[1]) m: 23 December 1829, Thornton Bradley, with Willis O'Bannon, bondsman. (Fauquier County)

117. NANCY A.[4] O'BANNON (Samuel[3]) m: Thomas W. Forrest, 10 Febr. 1823, Willis O'Bannon, bondsman. Thomas W. Forrest seems to have been a blacksmith — he was paid $19.90 from his father-in-law's estate for "blacksmith acct." in 1823. He also made several purchases at the sale of the estate. Nancy might have died before 1829 when he signed for his portion of the estate, with no indication that Nancy was joining in the receipt.

118. CRAVEN[4] O'BANNON (Samuel[3], John[2], Bryan[1]) was living in Shelby Co., KY. in 1823, when he appointed Willis O'Bannon his "true and lawful attorney" to receive his portion of their father's estate.

120. ENOCH[4] O'BANNON (Samuel[3]), b: 12 Oct. 1780; d: 30 Sept. 1820; m: 20 April 1808, Jane Hunt, with William Hunt as bondsman. Enoch O'Bannon died before his father, leaving seven children, all under the age of 21 years. On 26 July 1830, Edward Shacklett was appointed by the Fauquier Co. Court as guardian of the orphans. He entered into a bond with Absalom Hickerson as security in the amount of $500. The grave of Enoch O'Bannon is located on the land owned by Samuel O'Bannon, now being a portion of "Great Meadow" ("Home of the Gold Cup Races") near the Old Tavern. There is evidence of several other graves at the site, but Enoch's grave is the only one at which an engraved tombstone still exists.

ISSUE (O'BANNON):

244.   Elizabeth[5]
245.   Alfred[5], m: Frances Galleher
246.   Willis[5], m: Mary Mott, 1827, had: (1) Willis, Jr.
247.   Jane C.[5]
248.   Hiram[5], b: 19 Feb. 1818; d: 30 Mar. 1879, m: Mary
249.   William S.[5] buried, Edge Hill Cem., Charles Town, W.VA.
+ 250.   Enoch Washington[5]
251.   Wesley[5] (according to the late Claude A. O'Bannon there was a son named Wesley, who was lost at sea. This might be 241. William S. as there were no other children mentioned in the estate or guardian bond.)

135. PARMENAS BULLITT[5] O'BANNON (Joseph[4], John[3], John[2], Bryan[1]) b: ca: 1783; d: ca: 1835, Louisville, KY. He m: (1st) 26 Jan. 1807, Fauquier Co., VA., Catherine Johns(t)on; m: (2nd) 30 Sept. 1821, Shelby Co., KY., Mildred Roberts. His first wife, Catherine, was the dau. of Wilfred and Mary (Patton) Johnston. Under the terms of his father's will, in Fauquier County, Parmenas was to receive a "Negro lad named Nathan and $200" to be paid him as soon after his father's death as possible. Parmenas received the slave and $110 from his father's executor, Henry Mars Lewis, and claimed an additional $90 which Mr. Lewis refused to pay. Mr. Lewis contended that he had found a paper in which it was noted that Maj. Joseph O'Bannon had advanced Parmenas $90! It will be remembered that Mr. Lewis was the brother of Maj. O'Bannon's second wife, Elizabeth Mars Lewis. Parmenas and his Fishback nieces, daus. of his sister, Lydia, insisted that they were entitled to a portion of their deceased half-brother and half-sister, the children of Elizabeth (Lewis) O'Bannon. The Court ruled against their petition and Parmenas appealed the decision. On the appeal, Judge John Scott ruled in their favor in August 1835. The suit "O'Bannon vs. Waters," which settled Major O'Bannon's estate, was delayed by another suit, "Bullitt vs. O'Bannon's Admr." (File B-1]45, Circuit Superior Court). Burwell Bullitt (relationship to Parmenas B. O'Bannon is unknown) brought suit to redeem slaves Maj. O'Bannon had purchased from a Sheriff's sale of Bullitt's estate in 1800. Maj. O'Bannon had allegedly promised Bullitt that if the latter could repay him, Bullitt could redeem the slaves. Henry M. Lewis, the administrator, refused to honor the promise, declaring he knew nothing of it. Parmenas claimed that his father thought Bullitt would never be able to redeem the slaves and promised them to Parmenas and his sister Lydia Fishback — they did not have anything in writing either! The Court ruled against Lewis. The case continued on an appeal and was finally dropped in 1834, due to the death of Bullitt in KY. Parmenas B. O'Bannon was living in Shelby Co., KY. by 1820, with a large family. The following children might not be his entire family, nor is it certain by which marriage:

ISSUE (O'BANNON):

252. Mary E.[6], b: 1809; d: 16 Aug. 1857; m: 24 April 1827, Shelby Co., KY, Capt. John Field. Capt. John Field m: (2nd) _____ O'Bannon, a cousin of Mary, and moved, in 1862, to Texas.
253. Jane[6], m: John Applegate
254. Margaret[6], m: William Applegate
255. Helen[6], m: John Andrews
256. Mildred[6]
257. Lydia[6], m: 19 Sept. 1836, Jefferson Co., KY., Henry W. Hawes.

169. JANE H.[5] O'BANNON (John[4], John3 John[2], Bryan[1]) was the dau. of John and Frances (O'Bannon) O'Bannon. Called Fanny, Frances O'Bannon was the dau. of Thomas and Hannah (Barker) O'Bannon. Jane married 24 April 1826, Sylvester Welch, Jr., son of Sylvester and Ann (Glascock) Welch of Fauquier County. She is buried on the farm, known as "Flint Hill," adjoining the town of Marshall. The farm, now owned by George R. Thompson, was formerly owned by W. D. Stephenson. Sylvester Welch, Jr. married (2nd) Rachael (Satterwhite) Rector, widow of Ludwell Rector who is buried at Cool Spring United Methodist Church cemetery. Mr. Welch and Rachael

had the following children: Franklin Rush Welch (1835-1911); Morgan Sylvester Welch; Virginia Sanford Welch (1837-1927), who m: Enoch Milton Murray.

ISSUE (WELCH):

258.   Luther N.[6], 1827-1893, n. m.
259.   John N.[6], 1829-1856, n. m.
+ 260.   Frances A.[6], b: 28 Nov. 1832; d: 30 Dec. 1907

171. SUSANNAH[5] WATTS (Sarah[4] (#59); Sarah[3], John[2], Bryan[1]) married in Fauquier County, 13 Jan. 1802, Jeremiah Strother (His name is spelled incorrectly in the marriage bond: Strawther). He was a son of James and Jane (Gibson) Strother. Susannah (called Sukey) (Watts) Strother was named in her father's lease from George William Fairfax to a tract of land on the Rappahannock Mt. Range (near that part called Wild Cat Mt. and a portion of which is still called Strother's Mountain). She continued to live on the lease until her death, 11 Febr. 1855. She was born 2 Sept. 1779. The property changed hands several times during her lifetime and each time she had to defend, legally, her right to the part leased to her father, which included her mother and herself. Probably the longest continuous lawsuit in Fauquier County concerned the Watts-Strother lease, but Susannah was determined and fought those who would dispossess her until her death. Her heirs continued the fight, but lost. They finally purchased the property and her descendants (the Lee family) still own much of the property today (1993). Andrew O'Bannon (#18) and the Covert family, whom we have met previously, also had leases on the same Fairfax land. They tired of the constant changes of ownership and landlords' demands and moved away — to Kentucky and Missouri.

ISSUE (STROTHER):

261.   Hedgman F.[6], m: Frances Foley, 12 Nov. 1829, dau. of Enoch Foley.
262.   Enoch[6], n. m.
263.   Alexander[6], b: 30 Sept. 1807; d: 12 Apr. 1891, M: Maria Middleton, b: 1830; d: 1907, no issue. They are buried in the Strother-Lee Cemetery, near The Plains, VA.
264.   Octavia[6], d: 18 May 1879, aged 59 years. She m: (1st) Edward G. Richards and (2nd) John C. Dowell. No issue.
265.   Sarah Ann[6], m: Charles A. Chapman, 25 Anr. 1836. He inherited "Meadowville" farm from his father, which they sold and moved to Chariton Co., Missouri. Had: 1) George; 2) Strother, d: bef: 1874.

179. PRESLEY NEVILLE[5] O'BANNON (Thomas[4] (#76); William[3]) married 26 March 1827, Jane Sanford Welch, dau. of Sylvester and Ann (Glascock) Welch. She was born 10 Nov. 1801 and died 10 Nov. 1870. P. N. O'Bannon, nephew and namesake of his famous uncle, Lt. P. N. O'Bannon, was b: 14 Feb. 1803 and died 23 March 1835. He inherited "Flint Hill" farm from his father which his widow sold after his death. Jane S. (Welch) O'Bannon married, as her 2nd husband, James

Enoch Murray (1801-1870). They had two children: Alice Ann (1847-1939) and James Robert (1850-1934). Mr. Murray had children by a previous marriage.

ISSUE (O'BANNON):

266. Thomas Sylvester[6], b: 7 Sept. 1830; d: 23 July 1832. Buried with the family at "Flint Hill" farm, near Marshall, VA.

191. PRESLEY NEVILLE[5] JEFFRIES (Agnes[4] (#78) b: 1805; d: 1887; m: 30 April 1827, Nancy Utterback. They moved to Maysville, Mason Co., KY. where his sister, Sarah (Jeffries) Fishback lived.

ISSUE (JEFFRIES):

267. Mary Frances[6], b: 6 Sept. 1829
268. George William[6], b: 10 Sept. 1832
269 Sally Smith[6]

193. DRUCILLA[5] JEFFRIES (Agnes[4]) b: 5 Aug. 1811; d: 23 Sept. 1876, at Marshall, VA. She m: 3 Feb. 1841, Wilfred Neville Utterback (1816-1890). He m: (2nd), Nannie Lawrence, 5 Feb. 1880, a cousin of his first wife. Wilfred N. and Nannie (Lawrence) Utterback had one child, a dau., Drucilla, b: 1880; m: Edward S. Russell, of Marshall, VA.

ISSUE (UTTERBACK):

270. Henry Clay[6], b: 1843, m: Pattie Ann Payne. They had five chidren: 1) Lillian W.[7] (1872-1928); 2) Harriet Neville, b: 1874, m: Henry W. Speiden; 3) Wilfred M.[7] (1876-1887); 4) Clarence C.[7] (1881-1882); and 5) Andrew Withers[7], b: 1883, n.m.

The Utterback home, in Marshall, VA., is now owned by Mrs. Lou B. O'Bannon (Mrs.. John Norris O'Bannon, Sr.)

218. JAMES M.[5] O'BANNON (Bryant[4], William[3], John[2], Bryan[1]) married 1 January 1845, Lucy M. Lillard. They were married by Rev. Barnett Grimsley, a noted Baptist minister of Culpeper and Rappahannock Counties. He died in 1853 and his widow m: (2nd), 1885, Cornelius Smith, of Rappahannock County.

ISSUE (O'BANNON):

+ 271. Roberta[6]
+ 272. Presley Henry[6], b: 1849; d: 1933.

219. JOHN MAURICE[5] O'BANNON (Bryant[4], William[3]), b: 1800; d: 1870. Mr. O'Bannon was born in Rappahannock County and moved to Stafford County, near Falmouth. He married in 1830, Harriet Ann Corbin, b: 18 July 1813; d: 9 Jan. 1891, dau. of Jameson Corbin of Falmouth. In Dec. 1837 John M. O'Bannon purchased "Carlton" (known in the O'Bannon family as "Carlton Heights") from Rev. Cumberland George, who served as pastor of Jeffersonton Baptist Church in Culpeper Co. and Thumb Run Baptist Church in Fauquier Co., among other pastorates. "Mr.. O'Bannon provided the slave labor for loading and unloading the ships at Falmouth when it was a thriving shipping port." (Musselman, C. L.: STAFFORD COUNTY, VIRGINIA CEMETERIES (Stafford, 1983). The O'Bannon Cemetery is still preserved at "Carlton" and although probably the resting place of J. M. O'Bannon, there is no stone.

ISSUE (O'BANNON):

+ 273. Henry Clay[6]
  274. Nannie R.[6], b: 19 Feb. 1849; d: 23 May 1935, testate, Stafford Co., buried at "Carlton".
  275. Ellen A.[6], b: 8 Aug. 1846; d: 7 March 1937, buried at "Carlton", Stafford County, VA.
+ 276. Walter[6], b: 17 Sept. 1835; d: bef: 1900

220. WALTER C.[5] O'BANNON (Bryant[4], William[3]), b: ca: 1805; d: 1870. Married Elizabeth F. Eggborn (d: 1899), dau. of George Eggborn (1797-1848) and Amy (McQueen) Eggborn. He died "of heart disease, at his residence in the county of Culpeper, VA., aged 65 years. He was born and reared in the County of Rappahannock but settled and lived in the county of Culpeper." (Alexandria (VA.) Gazette, August, 1870).

ISSUE (O'BANNON):

  277. George Anna[6], b: 12 Apr. 1842, Boston Mills, VA.; d: 20 Nov. 1852, Boston Mills.
  278. Charles[6], b: 21 Nov. 1843, Boston Mills; d: 7 July 1860. "In Culpeper Co. on the 7th inst. Charles O'Bannon, only son of Walter O'Bannon, in the 17th year of his age." (Alexandria Gazette, 16 July 1860) His portrait, in oils, was in the possession of Mrs. William J. Smith, "Ashland Farms", Culpeper Co., VA.
  279. Laura[6], b: 26 Aug. 1845; Boston Mills; d: 18 Feb. 1847.
+ 280. Mary Elizabeth ("Mollie")[6], b: 1857; d: 1943.

221. JOSEPH(US)[5] O'BANNON (Bryant[4]), died in 1884, intestate, in Rappahannock County. He married, 1851, Margaret A. Deal. He died without issue in Rappahannock County, his wife, having predeceased him. To settle his estate Presley H. O'Bannon, a nephew, instituted a suit in the above county, styled "O'Bannon vs. Brady" (#401). Joseph died possessed of a lot of woodland and a tract of 30 acres, on which stood his home, near Rock Mills and a house and lot in the town of Salem (now Marshall) in Fauquier Co. which he had inherited from his father. The home and woodland, about 49 acres, in Rappahannock Co. was sold to John B. Brady in 1885. During his lifetime,

Joseph had sold several small lots in or near Salem (now Marshall), including the lot on which Trinity Episcopal Church now stands, in 1846. This land had come to Joseph from his father, Bryant, who inherited it from his father, William.

222. ANN (NANCY)[5] O'BANNON (Bryant[4]) married 2 March 1830, John Brady. The ceremony was performed by Rev. William F. Broaddus. (Culpeper Marriage Book 1, p. 99). Ann (O'Bannon) Brady was dead by 1885 when the suit, "O'Bannon vs. Brady", was filed by P. H. O'Bannon, adm'r. of Joseph O'Bannon. Her children are named in the Bill filed in the suit. There is a letter, dated 9 June 1961, filed in the suit, from Mrs. Henrietta A. Brady of Blantonia Plantation, Lorman, Mississippi, inquiring about the suit and a copy of James M. Settle's reply.

ISSUE (BRADY):

281.   Joseph[6]
282.   James[6]
283.   Bryant[6]
284.   Albert[6]
285.   William B.[6]
286.   Amanda[6]
287.   Bettie[6]
288.   Ann Eliza[6], m: Madison H. Thomas
289.   Sarah[6], m: Richard Hudnell

224. MARY A.[5] O'BANNON (Bryant[4], William[3], John[2], Bryan[1]) married 1853, Elder John H. Menefee, "a native of Page County, VA. He was born 23 Sept. 1820 and died 8 March 1897 .. Early in life he was convicted of sin and found peace and rest along by faith in Jesus .. was ordained to the gospel ministry, and for forty years proved a faithful soldier of Jesus. During the division of 1890 when the "Regular" Baptist or more generally and properly known "Burnham Baptists" were cut off by the old School Baptists on account of their doctrine and practice of human means in the salvation of sinners, Elder Menefee remained with the Old School Baptists and continued until the end, preaching salvation alone by the sovereign, eternal, unchangeable mercy of God .. he served Mill Creek, Brocks Gap and several other churches of the Ebenezer Association .." (Pittman, R. H.: BIOGRAPHICAL HISTORY OF PRIMITIVE OR OLD SCHOOL BAPTIST MINISTERS OF THE U. S. (c. 1909), p. 174).

225. CHARLES BRYANT[1]5 O'BANNON (Bryant[4], William[3]) married Amanda M. Eggborn, dau. of George Eggborn. He died in 1858 and she m: (2nd) 1861, George W. Rowles, who died testate in 1868.

ISSUE (O'BANNON):

+ 290.   Eggborn[6], b: February 1850.

250. ENOCH WASHINGTON[5] O'BANNON (Enoch[4], Samuel[3], John[2]) born 1820; m: Susan Smallwood, 17 December 1844, Loudoun Co., VA., dau. of Wesley Smallwood. They lived at Macsville, Loudoun Co. (near Middleburg) and are buried at Sharon Cemetery, Middleburg. He was a tinner at Macsville.

ISSUE (O'BANNON):

   291.   Susan J.[6], b: 1846; m: 13 Nov. 1873, Richard A. Sprouse, Loudoun Co., VA.
+ 292.   John Willis[6], 1847-1933
   293.   Mary R.[6], b: 1849; m: Ashford Weadon, widower, Loud. Co., VA., 23 June 1875. (Known as Beck)
   294.   Sarah E.[6], b: 1851
   295.   Georgiana[6], b: 1856 (might be Anne[6] who m: Smith German)
   296.   Gertrude[6], b: 1857, m: John W. Poston, 8 Aug. 1878, Loudoun County.
   297.   Kate H.[6], b: 1861, m: Wm. B. Poston, 20 Sept. 1877, Loudoun County.
   298.   William S.[6], b: 1864
+ 299.   Corbin M. L.[6], b: 7 Oct. 1866, Macsville, Loud. Co.
   300.   Enoch W.[6], 1853-1859, buried Sharon Cemetery
   301.   Anne[6], might be same as #287, Georgiana, who married Smith German and had: l) Ernest and 2) "Booty" German

260. FRANCES A.[6] WELCH (Jane H.[5], John[4], John[3], John[2]) was born 28 November 1832 and died 30 December 1907, at "Mountain View", between The Plains and Hopewell. She married, 18 February 1858, John Linton Combs, son of Burr and Catherine (Welch) Combs. J. L. Combs was born 11 Aug. 1827 and died 14 March 1878. Frances A. Welch and John L. Combs were first cousins. They are buried in the Marshall Cemetery, Marshall, VA.

ISSUE (COMBS):

302. Ada Patterson[7], b: 6 Jan. 1858; d: 2 Sept. 1918, n.m.
303. Beverly B.[7], b: 22 Aug. 1867; d: 1933, n. m.
304. Dixie Lee[7], b: 17 July 1861; d:
305. Jane Linton[7], b: 2 Aug. 1864; d: 14 Sept. 1918, m: Enoch Foley. She is buried at Marshall and he is buried at Antioch Baptist Church, near Waterfall, Pr. Wm. Co., VA. Had: 1) Lucille (1899-1980) m: (1st) Ralph Janoschka; m: (2nd) Ronald McLennan; 2) Elizabeth; 3) Ann.
306. Catherine C.[7], d: 25 Dec. 1958; n. m.
307. Virginia Elizabeth[7], b: 28 July 1876; d: 24 Oct. 1961; m: Leon Albert Warren, no issue.
308. Paul[7], b: 1875; d: 4 Jan. 1939, lived at Hopewell and buried at Marshall Cemetery, Marshall, VA.

271. ROBERTA[6] O'BANNON (James M.[5], Bryant[4], William[3]) married, 1873, Silas Lee Cooper.

ISSUE (COOPER):

309. Robert[7]
310. Henry O'Bannon[7], m: _____. Mrs. Cooper sponsored the first destroyer named for Lt. Presley N. O'Bannon, the O'BANNON (DD 177) when she was launched 28 February 1919 at the Potrero Plant of the Bethlehem Shipbuilding Corp. Henry O'B. Cooper was a member of the legal staff of the Southern Railway, Washington, D. C.

272. PRESLEY HENRY[6] O'BANNON (James M.[5], Bryant[4], William[3]) was born in Rappahannock Co., VA., 16 May 1848. Mr. O'Bannon lived at Sperryville where he was a merchant. He was proud of the fact that he was a cousin of William Jennings Bryan, through his mother, Lucy Mildred Lillard, and a grand-nephew of Lt. Presley N. O'Bannon, having been named for him. While at school Mr. O'Bannon enlisted in the 49th VA. Infantry, CSA, under Col. William Smith. Later he served in the 43rd VA. Cav. under the command of Col. John S. Mosby.

"Following his return home after the close of the War the young soldier attended Roanoke College to complete his education, and then went into the mercantile business .. A staunch Democrat, Mr. O'Bannon has been very active in his party, and for fifty years served as a member of the local school board. On May 14, 1879, Mr. O'Bannon married at Washington, VA., Anna

Josephine Miller, a dau. of Middleton and Anna Louise (Hubbs) Miller." He died in 1933 and Mrs. O'Bannon died in 1929.

ISSUE (O'BANNON):

311.   Louise Mildred[7], b: August 1881; d:

273. HENRY CLAY[6] O'BANNON (John Maurice[5], Bryant[4]) born 1842; m: Mary E. Frazier. The children listed below are listed in the Chancery Suit, "O'Bannon vs. Brady", Rappahannock Co., ca. 1890-1899 and the estate of Nannie Roy O'Bannon, Stafford Co., 18 June 1935. In both cases Henry C. O'Bannon is deceased.

ISSUE (O'BANNON):

312.   Henry Clay[7], dead by 1935
313.   Edwin Frazier[7], b: 7 Oct. 1872, lived in Washington, D. C.
314.   Nannie Lee[7], b: 1870; d: 12 Jan. 1964, in Washington, D. C. She was survived by F. Maury Cralle of Manhasset, N. Y. She was buried in the Congressional Cemetery, Washington.
315.   Carrie Bell[7], aged 51 in 1935, m: Geo. Cralle, res. (1935) Washington, D. C.
316.   Walter[7], b: 25 Oct. 1874; d: 31 Dec. 1956, buried Congressional Cemetery, Washington, D.C.
317.   Narcissa[7], aged 48 years, 1935, m: E. F. Kennedy, res: Washington, D. C. Mrs. Kennedy sponsored the second ship of the U. S. Navy to be named for Lt. P.N. O'Bannon, launched in 1942.

276. WALTER[6] O'BANNON (John Maurice[5], Bryant[4], William[3]) was born 9 Decemher 1835 at "Carlton Heights", Falmouth, VA. and died 12 May 1893. He married, 19 Nov. 1857, Martha Eliza Lucas, b: 5 May 1837; d: 27 March 1915. Martha E. Lucas was the daughter of Albert G. and Cornelia (Ennever) Lucas. Cornelia (Ennever) Lucas was a daughter of Joseph Ennever (1770-1848) and his wife, Lucy Latham. The Ennever family lived at "Stanstead", the home of the Hon. Charles Carter, son of Robert "King" Carter. According to the late George H. S. King, Joseph Ennever came to Virginia at the age of 17 and was scribe and bookkeeper to the executors of James Hunter (1722-1784) merchant and iron forge owner at Falmouth. Joseph Ennever was born at Dunkirk in French Flanders, 22 Jan. 1770. He married (1st) 8 April 1806, Fanny Potts, dau. of Richard Potts of King George County; she died without issue prior to her said father, Richard Potts, Sr. (ca. 1753-1823) who so states in his will. He married (2nd) in Stafford County, Lucy Latham. The Ennever- Lucas families are buried at "Stanstead", Stafford County.

Mr. O'Bannon was a very successful farmer. He tiled his own land and rented land to extend his farming. On one occasion, according to his grandson, Mr. J. Maurice O'Bannon of Woodville and Sperryville, he had on his own and rented land, over 300 acres of wheat. Nearing harvest time, the last of June or early July, the cradles were sharpened and laid out for the hands and sons to cut the crop. On evaluating the enormous task ahead, the story is that three sons left immediately for Texas! The next year Mr. O'Bannon purchased a wheat binder — but, too late, his sons had gone West!

ISSUE (O'BANNON):

318. John Maurice[7], b: 21 Oct. 1858; d: 11 March 1950, n.m.
+ 319. Albert Lucas[7], b: 26 March 1860; d: 30 July 1939
320. Henry Clay[7], b: 2 April 1862; d. yg.
321. Ellen Cornelia[7] (or Amelia), b: 10 Oct. 1864; d: 18 July 1943, n.m.
+ 322. William Oscar[7], b: 30 Dec. 1866
+ 323. Joseph Hill[7], b: 30 April 1869
324. Eva Gay[7], b: 13 Oct. 1871; d: 23 Jan. 1921. According to her obit. in the RELIGIOUS HERALD, she was a faithful and consistent member of the Sperryville Baptist Church and the W.M.U. She was ever willing and ready to help in any work she could do. A suiting resolution was made by a committee of the church, consisting of Mrs. J. Walton Wood, Mrs. Hugh Gore and Miss Annie Wood.
325. Walter Herbert[7], b: 20 April 1874; d: 9 Sept. 190S, n. m.
+ 326. Lillian[7], b: 11 March 1877
+ 327. Cabell Preston[7], b: 26 April 1880

280. MARY ELIZABETH[6] O'BANNON (Walter C.[5], Bryant[4]) called "Mollie", she was born 22 Sept. 1857 at Boston Mills, Culpeper Co., VA. and died 26 December 1943 at the home of her daughter, Elizabeth R. Durant. She married 22 Oct. 1874, Hugh Mercer Smith, b: 11 Aug. 1850, son of Cornelius and Tabitha (Browning) Smith, Laurel Mills, Rappahannock Co., VA. He died 7 May 1897 at "Clover Hill", Rappahannock Co. They were the parents of twelve children. NOTE: Here the presentation of the descendants of Mary E. (O'Bannon) Smith will change to keep the huge progeny together — only the children will retain the continuous numbering of the descendants.

ISSUE (SMITH):

328. Elizabeth Russell[7] Smith, b: 8 Sept. 1875, Boston Mills; d: 18 Feb. 1956, Florida; bur. 20 Feb. 1956, Culpeper, VA.; m: 22 Nov. 1899, John Griffin Durant, b: 22 Sept. 1860; d: 9 March 1948; both bur. Fairview Cemetery, Culpeper.
   Issue:
   1. Oliver[8] Durant, II, b: 23 Oct. 1900, "The Hill", Boston, VA.; m: (1) 5 Sept. 1925, Louisa Yates, divorced; m: (2) Patsey ____; divorced; remarried (3) Patsey ____; re-divorced Patsey and remarried (4) Louisa Yates, his first wife; divorced her a second time and married (5) as his third wife, 22 April 1955, Emily Shultz, b: 15 June 1903. He was married five times; but had only three wives!! Issue:
      1. Mary Gertrude[9] Durant, b: 13 July 1928, Washington, D.C., m: 5 Sept. 1951, George Rodman Lucas, b: 13 Jan. 1928. Issue:
         1. Sharon Scott Lucas[10], b: 9 July 1956; m: 2 Sept. 1979, Clyde Porter.

2. Louisa Perry[9] Durant, b: 1 Dec. 1932, D.C.; m: 5 Sept. 1953, Karl Jorss, b: 4 Aug. 1927. Issue:
 1. Karl[10] Jorss, b: 15 Dec. 1955
 2. Perry Scott[10], Jorss, b: 8 April 1962
 3. Christopher Fantaine[10] Jorss, b: 25 July 1963

2. John Griffin[8] Durant, Jr., b: 9 Dec. 1901, "The Hill", Boston, VA.; m.(l) 1 June 1922, Kitty Morefield, b: 1 Oct. 1905; d: 11 Dec. 1966; div. m: (2) Pearl Meadows, divorced; m:(3) 11 May 1939, Virginia Rothwell, b: 25 Nov. 1909. Issue by first marriage:
1. William Oliver[9] Durant, b: 9 Dec. 1924; d: April 1929
2. John Lee[9] Durant, m: Jane Elizabeth Mather, b: 11 Nov. 1923. Issue:
 1. John Griffin[10] Durant, III, b: 22 Jan. 1947; m: 14 Feb. 1970, Sallie Utley.
 2. Stephen Lee[10] Durant, b: 6 July 1948; m: (1) 4 May 1968, Judith Hampe, b: 19 Jan. 1949, div.; m: (2) 1974, ____ Meadows. Issue, 1st marriage:
  1. Melissa Lynn[11] Durant, b: 28 Oct. 1970.

329. Mary Tabitha[7] Smith, b: 23 May 1877, Boston Mills, VA.; d: Univ. of VA. Hospital, Charlottesville, 15 Feb. 1943; m: 25 April 1901, Robert Middleton Menefee, b: 10 June 1876; d: 13 Aug. 1932, Univ. of VA. Hosp. from injury on a horse. Issue:
1. Robert Mercer[8] Menefee, b: 1 July 1902; d: 16 Dec. 1966, Culpeper, VA.; m: 12 June 1937, Ann Keyser. Issue:
 1. Robert Mercer[9] Menefee, Jr. b: 15 July 1938
 2. Edward Lynn[9] Menefee, b: 26 Dec. 1944; m: 6 Jan. 1968, Shirley Ann Stevens. Issue:
  1. Robert Lynn[10] Menefee, b: 22 May 1970
2. Mary Helen[8] Menefee, m: 26 Aug. 1939, M. P. Watkins, Jr., b: 25 Aug. 1903. Issue:
 1. Mary Helen[9] Watkins, b: 5 Nov. 1944; m: 10 Aug. 1969, Gerald Smith. Issue:
  1. Brian Stanley[10] Smith, b: 25 Feb. 1974
  2. Marc David[10] Smith, b: 20 May 1975

330. Walter O'Bannon[7] Smith, b: 18 July 1878, Boston Mills, VA.; d: 18 March 1957, Spokane, Wash.; bur. Fairview Cem., Culp., VA.; m: 5 Nov. 1919, Mattie Breckenridge, b: 4 Jan. 1899, of Liberty, Mo. Issue:
1. Hugh Breckenridge[8] Smith, b: 2 Sept. 1920; m: 22 Oct. 1949, Excelsior Springs, Mo., Dolores Rose Heckel, b: 21 Aug. 1928. Issue:
 1. Dolores Gene[9] Smith, b: 3 March 1954
 2. Hugh Breckenridge[9] Smith, Jr., b: 9 May 1959
 3. Jeffrey Walter[9] Menasco, b: 24 Oct. 1959, Encino, Calif.
2. Dixie Lorene[8] Smith, b: 4 Sept. 1924; m: 14 Oct. 1949, Liberty, Mo., Laurence Clifton Menasco, b: 21 Sept. 1923, Clark Co., Miss. Issue:
 1. Lawrence Clifton[9] Menasco, Jr., b: 22 April 1953, Albuquerque, N. Mex.

2.   William Wyatt[9] Menasco, b: 7 Sept. 1954, Lancaster, Calif.
3.   Jeffrey Walter[9] Menasco, b: 24 Oct. 1959, Encino, Calif.

331.   Corrie Lee[7] Smith, b: 22 Feb. 1880, Boston Mills, VA.; d: 4 March 1972, San Antonio, Texas; aged 92, bur. Huntsville, Texas; m: 27 Aug. 1902, Luther Eastham, b: 26 April 1880. Issue:
1.   Corrie Lee[8] Eastham, b: 5 June 1913; d: 1974; m: 10 Oct. 1931, Lawrence O. Brown, b: 7 June 1908. Issue:
    1.   Judith Suzanne[9] Brown, b: 25 April 1939; m: 6 Sept. 1958, Thomas Fowler Welker, b: 15 Feb. 1938. Issue:
       1.   Lee Anne Elizabeth[10] Welker, b: 8/25/1959
       2.   Leynette Lynn[10] Welker, b: 2/18/1965
    2.   Joan Dianne[9] Brown, b: 9 Aug. 1941; M; 6 Aug 1960, Donald Ray Quick, b: 23 Sept. 1938.
       1.   Deborah Dee[10] Quick, b: 1 Aug. 1964
       2.   Lori Lane[10] Quick, b: 16 Dec. 1967

332.   Lucy Mildred[7] Smith, b: 29 Sept. 1881, Boston Mills, VA.; d: 16 Sept. 1936, Washington, D.C., bur. Fairview Cem., Culp. m: (1) 24 June 1903, R. H. Wooters; m: (2) ____ Hunter. Issue, 1st. m:
1.   Corrie Mildred[8] Wooters, b: 16 Nov. 1910; m: 3 Nov. 1928, Addison Davis, Jr., b: 30 July 1908. Issue:
    1.   Tadd[9] Davis, III, b: 30 Sept. 1929. Issue:
       1.   Tadd[10] Davis, IV, b: 13 Dec. 1956
       2.   Murray[10] Davis, b: 4 March 1959
    2.   Mary Elizabeth[9] Davis, b: 10 Feb. 1932

333.   Hugh Mercer[7] Smith, Jr., b: 9 Aug. 1883, Boston Mills, VA.; d: 18 Jan. 1927, Texas, buried in Texas; m: in Texas, Blanche Sims. Issue:
1.   Hugh Mercer[8] Smith, III, b: 18 May 1917
2.   John Seams[8] Smith, b: 12 Nov. 1923

334.   Rebecca Miller[7] Smith, b: 22 Nov. 1885, "Clover Hill", Rappahannock Co.; d: 5 Mar. 1941, bur. Fairview Cem., Culpeper. Her mother found her dead in bed. She m: 18 Dec. 1907, Carroll Burgess, d: 13 Dec. 1944. Issue:
1.   Elizabeth Lee[8] Burgess, b: 31 July 1909; d: 3 March 1981; M: 14 July 1928, Ed Turner. Issue:
    1.   Ed[9] Turner, Jr., b: 15 Nov. 1929; m: 13 July 1957, Rebecca Armistead Gill of "Remlik Hall", Remlik, VA. Issue:
       1.   Elizabeth Davidson[10] Turner, b: 12/21/60
       2.   Ernest Dailey[10] Turner, IV, b: 9/9/63
2.   Carroll[8] Burgess, Jr., b: 2 Apr. 1913; d: 22 Oct. 1925, d.s.p.

335. Frankie English[7] Smith, b: 6 Aug. 1887, "Clover Hill", d: 25 Jan. 1961, bur. Fairview Cem. She m: (1) 28 Aug. 1907, Frank Edmiston, b: 5 Apr. 1875; d: after swimming, 18 July 1922; m: (2) 15 Dec. 1923, Carroll Menefee, b: 21 July 1876; d: 13 Dec. 1944. Issue, 1st. marr:

1. Jane Elizabeth[8] Emiston, b: 2 Oct. 1909; d: 27 June 1974, Savannah, Ga.; bur. Fairview Cem.; m: (1) 6/6/1926, James Williams, div.; m: (2) 11/30/1933, Andrew Preston Jarvis, div.; m: (3) 2/27/1954, Minor Lewis, Jr., b: 11/6/1906. Issue, 2nd marr:

    1. Preston[9] Jarvis, Jr., b: 7/8/1937; m: 7/24/1964, Beverly Black, b: 12/29/1940, Issue:

        1. Mary Ellen[10] Jarvis, b: 7/1/1967

    2. Frank Edmiston[9] Jarvis, b: 1/5/1944; m: Janet Taylor, b: 2/31/1941. Issue:

        1. Wade Edmiston[10] Jarvis, b: 5/5/1966

        2. Lisa[10] Jarvis, b: 12/18/1963

Issue, 2nd marr.:

2. Carroll[8] Menefee, Jr., b: 7 June 1926; m: Joyce Farrar, b: 10 June 1931, div. and both remarried. Issue:

    1. Larry[9] Menefee, b: 19 June 1954

    2. Suzanne Elizabeth[9] Menefee, b: 1 Nov. 1956

    3. Mary Frances[9] Menefee, b: 23 July 1959

336. Georgia Allie[7] Smith, b: 21 Nov. 1889, d: same day.

337. Charles William Jacob[7] Smith, b: 25 Sept. 1890, "Clover Hill,"; d: 22 Jan. 1977, aged 86. He married 27 Jan. 1915, St. Joseph, Mo., Myra Elizabeth Griffin, b: 14 March 1892, dau. of Frederick Blackford and Frankie Clayton Griffin. Mrs. Smith lived at "Ashland Farms", Culpeper, VA. Issue:

1. William Jacob[8] Smith, Jr., b: 24 Mar. 1916; d: 24 May 1969, bur. Fairview Cem.; m: (1) 5/15/1939, Mary Crandall of Warrenton, VA.; div. 1962; m: (2) 1/19/1965, Helen Swartz, b: 9 May 1914. Issue, 1st. marr.:

    1. Gregory Allen[9] Smith, b: 4/1.1940, "Ashland Farms", m: 6/15/1963, Doris Ann Estes, b: 2 Sept. 1930. Issue:

        1. Allen Todd[10] Smith, b: 29 Dec. 1968

        2. Tammy Gale[10] Smith, b: 12 Aug. 1971

    2. Kenneth Wayne[9] Smith, b: 8 Aug. 1944, Warrenton, m: 5 June 1971, Nancy Richardson, b: 12 Aug. 1949. Issue:

        1. Kenneth Scott[10] Smith, b: 16 Apr. 1973

    3. Emily Ilene[9] Smith, b: 18 March 1947, Warrenton m: 3/6/1971, Richmond, Dwight Moody

    4. Valerie Elizabeth[9] Smith, b: 6 May 1948, Warrenton, VA., m: 12 June 1966, Curtis Myers, Jr., b: 12 June 1946. Issue:

        1. Curtis[10] Myers, III, b: 19 April 1971

2. Frankie Clayton[8] Smith, b: 12 April 1918; m: (1) 7/8/1941, Edwin A. Yandell, Jr., b: 28 Nov. 1915; d: 28 Nov. 1971, div., 1953; m: (2) 20 Oct. 1956, John R. Wilson, b: 29 Oct. 1917; d: 7 Feb. 1972. Issue, 1st marriage:

1.   Edwin Addington[9] Yandell, III (Name changed to John R. Wilson, Jr., and adopted by John R. Wilson, Sr.) b: 29 Nov. 1947, Brooklyn, N. Y.; m: (1) 18 Dec. 1971, Allison Graves, b: 4 Sept. 1951; dau. of V. M. and Carolyn Graves of Culpeper, div.; m: (2) 18 Oct. Terry Wagner.

Issue, 2nd marriage:

2.   Sharon Clayton[9] Wilson, b: 25 Nov. 1957.

3.   Myra Elizabeth[8] Smith, b: 12 Jan. 1920; m: 18 March 1944, Warner Thompson Ferguson, b: 18 Jan. 1913. Issue:

    1.   Warner T.[9] Ferguson, Jr., b: 28 March 1947; m: 28 July 1973, Stephanie Tooles, b: 30 July 1950. Issue:

        1.   Andrew Christopher[10] Ferguson, b: 10 April 1980, Wentheine, Germany

        2.   Ronald Stephen[10] Ferguson, b: 4 Feb. 1951; m: 26 July 1975, Nancy Maloney

4.   Harold Stephen[8] Smith, b: 9 Dec. 1922, killed in auto accident in Warrenton, VA., 23 March 1947; m: 17 Jan. 1946, Kitty Whitehurst, also killed in same accident.

338.   Laura Josephine[7] Smith, b: 26 July 1893, "Clover Hill", Rappahannock Co., VA., d: 26 Nov. 1958

339.   Cornelius[7] Smith, b: 30 March 1895, "Clover Hill"; d: 14 Sept. 1965, Veterans' Hospital, Hampton, VA., bur. National Cemetery, Culpeper.

The above lineages of the descendants of Mollie (O'Bannon) Smith courtesy of Katherine F. Weaver from information in possession of Frankie (Smith) Wilson.

290. EGGBORN BRYANT[6] O'BANNON (Charles B.[5], Bryant[4]) was born in February 1850 and died at his home near Eggbornville, Culpeper Co., VA. on 14 January 1922 of pneumonia. His funeral services were held at the Salem Baptist Church by Rev. G. W. Cox, his pastor, and he was buried in the church cemetery. He married Willie Hannah Thomas of Madison County, the dau. of Capt. William Thomas. She died 28 February 1921, at the age of 63 years.

ISSUE (O'BANNON):

340.   John Henry[7], d. in infancy
341.   Pearl[7], d. at age of 3 or 4
+ 342.   Charles William[7], b: 18 Dec. 1877
343.   Sandy Thomas[7], b: 8 Nov. 1879; d: 8 Dec. 1908, n.m.
344.   Jacob T.[7], b: Jan. 1883 (known as Jake) M; Genevieve Newland. They lived in California.
+ 345.   Walter George[7], b: Jan. 1885 (according to the 1900 Census); d: 27 August 1982.
346.   Judson Browning[7], b: 26 March 1886; d: 1 Mar. 1956, m: Ollie G. Curtis. Issue: 1) Russell Mae; 2) Billy; 3) Dorothy. They lived near Rixeyville, VA.
+ 347.   Jackson Stuart[7], b: 26 March 1888

+ 348.   Delores Margaret[7], b: June 1895
  349.   Eggborn Bradford[7], b: Aug. 1891; d: 19 July 1971; m: Reba J. _____. They lived in Dayton, Ohio. Had two daughters: 1) Mrs. Irvin Wohlgemuth and 2) Mrs. Robert Murphy, both of Dayton, Ohio.
+ 350.   Richard Harry Lee[7]
  351.   Linwood Davis[7] (known as Sam or Samuel), m: Ethel Norris.

292. JOHN WILLIS[6] O'BANNON (Enoch W.[5], Enoch[4], Samuel[3]) married 13 December 1871, Josephine Ballard, dau. of Joseph and Maria L. Ballard. She was born in Loudoun Co., VA. Mr. O'Bannon was a farmer in the Marshall area and both he and his wife are buried in the Marshall Cemetery. After his retirement, Mr. O'Bannon lived with his daughter and son-in-law, Mr. & Mrs. Harry H. Pearson, near Marshall.

ISSUE (O'BANNON):

+ 352.   Ernest William[7], b: 30 Oct. 1872; d: 29 March 1919.
+ 353.   Florence S.[7], b: 6 July 1878; d: 4 June 1951
+ 354.   Annie J.[7], b: 25 May 1880; d: 20 Aug. 1934
  355.   May A.[7], b: 1882; d: 1951, m: Walter A. Jones (1882-1956)
+ 356.   James Keith[7], b: 1883; d: 1965
  357.   Sarah L.[7], b: 6 Jan. 1885;
+ 358.   Harry Lee[7], b: 1888; d: 1960; m: Annie Wines, b: 1890.
  359.   Agnes[7], m: Berry Pearson; she was born 15 Sept. 1889
  360.   Carrie L.[7], b: 11 Feb. 1896; m: Harry H. Pearson. They had one dau.: Elizabeth, m: Archie J. Roberts, b: 10 Jan. 1914; d: 2 July 1982, had: 1) Patricia Roberts, m: (1) Howard C. Patton, Jr., div.; m: (2) Wilson Ramey, Jr.

299. CORBIN M. L.[6] O'BANNON (Enoch W.[5], Enoch[4], Samuel[3]) was born 29 October 1866 at Macsville, Loudoun Co., near Middleburg. According to his obituary in the Fairfax Herald, 19 Feb. 1940, he died "at his home on the Little River Pike, one of the oldest residents of the Pender neighborhood" on 11 February. "Mr.. O'Bannon had been engaged in farming and at one time was the proprietor of a blacksmith shop. He is survived by his wife, Mrs. Mary E. O'Bannon and one son, Cecil O'Bannon. Funeral services were held from Money & King Funeral Home in Vienna .. with the Rev. R. Carl Maxwell, pastor of the Fairfax Methodist Church officiating. Burial was in the Fairfax Cemetery." There is a tombstone at Mr. O'Bannon's grave, but none at the graves of his wives, if they are buried there too. He married, first, Georgia Smallwood and, second, Mary Elizabeth Simpson. She was a native of Pleasant Valley, Fairfax County, the dau. of R. F. Simpson — they were married 23 June 1917. The marriage license in Fairfax Co. states that he was 50 years of age and she was 37 and at the time he was a carpenter.

ISSUE (O'BANNON) — 1st Marriage:

+ 361.   Cecil Corbin[7], b: 4 Nov. 1888; d: 7 Jan. 1967.

319. ALBERT LUCAS[7] O'BANNON (Walter[6], John M.[5], Bryant[4]) born 26 March 1860; d: 30 July 1939. He married 6 Jan. 1895, Lila Byrd Hull, b: 20 Oct. 1867; d: 9 Feb. 1950. They lived in Loudoun County, VA. and are buried at Sharon Cemetery, Middleburg, VA.

ISSUE (O'BANNON):

362. Lizzie Clare[8], b: 22 Oct. 1895; d: 1971. She lived with her uncle's family at Woodville, Rappahannock County, VA.

322. WILLIAM OSCAR[7] O'BANNON (Walter[6], John Maurice[5]) born 30 December 1866; m: 7 Dec. 1892, Laura Northcutt of Bastrop County, Texas, and moved to Hamilton, Texas. Mr. and Mrs. O'Bannon celebrated their 60th wedding anniversary just a few days before Mrs. O'Bannon was stricken with a heart attack. She was a member of the Church of Christ.

ISSUE (O'BANNON):

363. William Welter[8], b: 2 Sept. 1893
364. Oscar Lee[8], b: 16 Jan. 1895
365. Robert[8], b: 21 Oct. 1898
366. Preston[8], b: 20 March 1903
367. Lillian Eleanor[8], b: 28 April 1906
368. Hazel Opal[8], b: 31 May 1910
369. Foy[8], b: 8 July 1912

323. JOSEPH HILL[7] O'BANNON (Walter[6], John Maurice[5], Bryant[4]) was born 30 April 1869 and died 26 June 1955. He m: (1st) Bertha Miller who died in 1918. He married (2nd) Catherine Kelley ("Rena") Armstrong, dau. of Ringgold and Ella (Miller) Armstrong. The O'Bannon family lived at "Clover Hill', near Woodville, where Mr. O'Bannon died. They were members of the Woodville Baptist Church. "The O'Bannons lived at "Clover Hill," which had been built by the Slaughters around the time of the Revolution. Cousin Rena O'Bannon was a granddaughter of Sarah Catherine Slaughter Armstrong, and thus a direct descendant of the Slaughters of "Clover Hill." (Armstrong Genealogy).

ISSUE (O'BANNON):

370. Joseph Hill[8], Jr., b: 12 Dec. 1921; d: 15 Dec. 1921
+ 371. John Maurice[8],III, b: 4 July 1923.

326. LILLIAN[7] (Lilly) O'BANNON (Walter[6], John Maurice[5]) married at "Carlton Heights", near Falmouth, VA., 6 Oct. 1914, to Samuel Burroughs Barber. They lived near Goldvein, VA. and after

Mr. Barber's death, Mrs. Barber moved to Woodville. She was an early O'Bannon genealogist of the Culpeper, Rappahannock and Stafford County brances of the family.

ISSUE (O'BANNON):

+ 372.   Martha Wallace⁸, b: 3 Dec. 1916

327. CABELL PRESTON⁷ O'BANNON (Walter⁶, John Maurice⁵) born 26 April 1880; d: 12 Sept. 1921. He married Cora Barrett in Texas and lived at Crockett, Texas where he was a merchant. A long and warm obituary appeared in the Houston County, Texas newspaper at the time of his death, ending with these words, "The Times feels like there is nothing it can say regarding the past of this good man that is not already known by our people. .. in his death we have lost one of our best friends .." Mr. and Mrs. O'Bannon had no children.

342. CHARLES WILLIAM⁷ O'BANNON (Eggborn B.⁶, Charles B.⁵, Bryant⁴, William³, John², Bryan¹) born 18 Dec. 1877; d: 2 Aug. 1970. He m: 14 March 1900, Mildred Carolyn Pulliam. She was born 26 Feb. 1880 and died 24 Jan. 1960. They lived near Boston, Culpeper County, VA.

ISSUE (O'BANNON):

+ 373.   Silas Lillard⁸, b: 10 April 1901; d: 16 Jan. 1982
  374.   Elizabeth Duncan⁸, b: 1 Feb. 1903; m: George William Partlow, b: 16 Apr. 1881; d: 2 Jan. 1962. Buried, Fairview Cem., Culpeper. Issue: 1) Wm. O'B.⁹ Partlow, b: 14 April 1928.
  375.   Mary Samson⁸, b: 27 May 1905
  376.   Virginia Davis⁸, b: 15 April 1907; d: 16 Nov. 1981; m: _____ Rosenberger. No issue.
+ 377.   Alexander Thomas⁸, b: 19 Dec. 1911; m: Doris Virginia Button.
+ 378.   Laura Margaret⁸, b: 10 Jan. 1923
+ 379.   Emily Bradford⁸, b: 5 Nov. 1925
  380.   Lucy Coleman⁸, m: Burl Frank Cannon. Issue: 1) Burl F. Cannon, Jr. and 2) Donald Coleman Cannon.
  381.   Carolyn Eggborn⁸, m: James Robert Bowen. Issue: 1) Elizabeth J. Bowen and 2) Michael Bowen.

345. WALTER GEORGE⁷ O'BANNON (Eggborn B.⁶, Charles B.⁵) born 22 Jan. 1885; d: 27 August 1982. He m: (1ˢᵗ) Frances Merriman Payne, dau. of George R. and Mary E. (Fant) Payne of Rixeyville, VA. She was b: 11 Oct. 1888 and was married 25 Sept. 1907. He moved to Washington in 1917 and was a Pullman conductor between Washington and Chicago and retired in 1955. He was a member of Broadview Baptist Church, Temple Hills, Maryland. Buried at Fairview Cem., Culpeper. He m: (2ⁿᵈ) his first wife's sister, Nellie George (Payne) Koontz, widow of Clarence Koontz. She was born 25 Dec. 1891 and died in 1977. No children by second wife.

ISSUE (O'BANNON):

382.   George Payne[8], b: 9 June 1909; d: 12 June 1927
383.   Nellie Louise[8], b: 21 June 1923; d: Jan. 1926
384.   Frances Elizabeth[8], b: 24 Nov. 1924; d: by 1982, m: James Burr Russell, b: 19 Oct. 1921. Issue: 1) George T.[9] Russell and 2) Michael Duane[9] Russell, b: 6 March 1947.

347. JACKSON STUART[7] O'BANNON (Eggborn B.[6]) born 26 March 1888; d: 10 March 1944; m: Lucy Mary Downer, 2 Dec. 1916. She was b: 5 May 1887 and d: 15 Sept. 1923.

ISSUE (O'BANNON):

385.   Annie Thomas[8], b: 8 May 1918; m: G. Stuart Hamm, Jr., 1 May 1948. Lived at Charlottesville, VA. (1961) Issue: 1) Gay Stuart Hamm, b: 19 Nov. 1955.
386.   Robert Eggborn[8], b: 12 May 1920, m: Anna Mildred Kabicek, dau. of Frank & Mary (Barta) Kabicek, b: 24 Oct. 1920 in Bad Nauheim, Germany, 19 July 1947. Issue: 1) Vicki Anne[9] O'Bannon, b: 12 July 1949; 2) Robert Allan[9] O'Bannon, b: 30 Apr. 1951 and 3) Michael Scott[9] O'Bannon, b: 8 Nov. 1954.

348. DOLORES M.[7] O'BANNON (Eggborn B.[6], Charles B.[5]) born 26 June 1892; M; 23 July 1912, James William Fletcher, b: 4 Jan. 1863; d: 6 April 1936. He was a son of Alpheus E. and Tabitha Browning (Johnson) (Wheatley) Fletcher. Alphas E. Fletcher was a son of William H. and Harriet (Lake) Fletcher of "Shirland Hall", Atoka, Fauquier Co., VA.

ISSUE (FLETCHER):

387.   Willie Sarah[8] (or Willie Mae), b: 28 Dec. 1913; d: 12 Oct. 1935; m. 12 Sept. 1935, Herbert Randolph Wood, b: 24 Nov. 1914.
388.   Tabitha Margaret[8], b: 21 Sept. 1916; m: 7 June 1941, Alwinus Van Niekerk (b: 9 June 1911). They were married on board a ship taking them to his home in South Africa.
389.   Meta Lake[8], b: 16 Jan. 1918; M: 1 May 1943, Wm. C. Phillips, b: 9 June 1919.
390.   James Lee[8], b: 3 Aug. 1923; m: Iris Kathleen Pridmore, 31 March 1945. Issue: 1) Margaret Ann[9] Fletcher, b: 10 April 1946 and 2) James Lee[9] Fletcher, b: 4 Nov. 1952.
391.   Helen Ann[8], b: 26 July 1925; m: 25 July 1945, Gordon Lee Worsham, b: 24 Aug. 1918. Issue: 1) William Donnelly[9] Worsham, b: 22 Oct. 1946; 2) Ronald Lee[9] Worsham, b: 25 Jan. 1948; 3) Merrill James[9] Worsham, b: 14 Dec. 1950; 4) Sue Ann[9] Worsham, b: 18 March 1952; 5) Mark Philip[9] Worsham, b: 15 Mar. 1956; 6) Alan Wayne[9] Worsham, b: 12 Apr. 1959; 7) Stewart Edward[9] Worsham, B: 15 Nov. 1960; 8) Nita Dolores[9] Worsham, b: 1 May 1964.
392.   Evelyn Jane[8], b: 12 Oct. 1931; m: 28 July 1950, George Edward Scott, Jr., b: 26 March 1931. Issue: 1) Geo. Edward[9] Scott, III, b: 20 Aug. 1953; 2) Steven Michael[9] Scott, b: 29 Oct. 1956; 3) James Patrick[9] Scott, b: 14 Nov. 1958 and 4) Terri Lynn[9] Scott, b: 24 Oct. 1962.

350. RICHARD HARRY LEE[7] O'BANNON (Eggborn B.[6], Charles B.[5]) was born 26 July 1895 and died in May 1976. He married 16 February 1924, Helen Bowers Thomas, b: 16 Dec. 1901. For some years the O'Bannons lived in Falls Church, VA. He retired to Culpeper in 1972 after serving as superintendent of maintenance at Doctors' Hospital in Washington, D. C. He was buried at Fairview Cemetery, Culpeper. Mrs. O'Bannon still lives (1991) in their home on South East Street in Culpeper. She has been active in many social and patriotic organizations and is a member of the Culpeper Baptist Church.

ISSUE (O'BANNON):

+ 393.   Betty Thomas[8], b: 20 June 1932
+ 394.   Richard H. L.[8], Jr., b: 14 October 1936

352. ERNEST WILLIS[7] O'BANNON (John Willis[6], Enoch W.[5], Enoch[4], Samuel[3]) born 30 October 1872; d: 29 March 1919; m: Lillian (Lillie) Leonard. Mr. O'Bannon was a farmer.

ISSUE (O'BANNON):

+ 395.   Claude Aaron[8], b: 11 Aug. 1896; d: 5 May 1964
  396.   Mary Josephine[8], m: 3 Dec. 1923, Fauquier Co., Bryan G. Yates. Lived in Warrenton. Issue: 1) Mrs. George Goff and 2) Mrs. Stuart Bryant.
  397.   Evvie[8], b: 19 Aug. 1898; d: 22 Oct. 1978, m: (as his 2nd wife) John E. Anderson, d: 17 Aug. 1960. He is buried at Fairfax Cemetery, Fairfax, VA. and she is buried with her parents at the Marshall Cemetery.

353. FLORENCE SEREPTA[7] O'BANNON (John Willis[6]) m: 28 December 1894, William Walter Pearson, b: 21 Oct. 1872; d: 5 April 1942. Mr. Pearson was, for many years, a deputy sheriff of Fauquier County.

ISSUE (PEARSON):

+ 398.   Emma Elizabeth[8], b: 25 Nov. 1895
+ 399.   Eva Josephine[8], b: 18 Feb. 1897
+ 400.   Ada Virginia[8], b: 9 Nov. 1898
  401.   Morris Albert[8], b: 15 Nov. 1900; died at 6 months
+ 402.   Walter William[8], b: 5 March 1902; d: 19 Oct. 1991
  403.   Infant _____[8] b: 14 Nov. 1904, d: at birth
+ 404.   Rena Marie[8], b: 13 Jan. 1908
  405.   Catherine Carrington[8], b: 29 Sept. 1909; d: 1989; m: Darius (Mike) Finley, 15 Feb. 1935. Lived at Delaplane and Marshall. No issue.
+ 406.   Alma Beatrice[8], b: 4 March 1912

+ 407.   Susie Gertrude[8], b: 22 July 1913
  408.   Edward Ambler[8], b: 27 Sept. 1916; m: 12 April 1946, Mary (Birdie) Heflin. Issue: 1) Michael[9]

354. ANNIE J.[7] O'BANNON (John Willis[6]) married 1897, Joseph A. Pearson (known as "Bub"), b: 12 Dec. 1875; d: 12 July 1968. Mr. Pearson was a farmer. They are buried at the Orlean Cemetery, Orlean, VA.

ISSUE (PEARSON):

409.   Beulah[8], m: _____ Jones
410.   Elsie[8], m: _____ Kirby
411.   Mabel[8], m:
412.   Annabell[8], m: _____ Ash. No issue.
413.   Julia[8], m: _____ McWhorter
414.   Channie[8]
415.   Tacie Marie[8], m: William Kines. Issue: 1) Phyllis[9] Kines.
416.   Carroll[8], m: _____ Putnam
417.   Ethel[8], m: _____ Cornwell
418.   Helen[8], m: Ray Pearson. Issue: 1) Michael[9] Pearson
419.   Rae[8], m: _____ Crabtree

356. JAMES KEITH[7] O'BANNON (John Willis[6], Enoch W.[5], Enoch[4], Samuel[3], John[2], Bryan[1]) married Elizabeth Pearson, daughter of Albert A. and Josephine Pearson, 31 August 1905, Fauquier County, VA. Mr. O'Bannon was born 16 Nov. 1883 and died at Warrenton, VA. 21 March 1965, having lived his entire life in Fauquier County. He was a retired farmer. Mr. and Mrs. O'Bannon are buried at Leeds Cemetery, Hume, VA. After Mrs. O'Bannon's death in 1954, Mr. O'Bannon came to Marshall to make his home with his son and daughter-in-law J. Norris and Lou B. O'Bannon. A few weeks of "rest" were too many for a man as active as Mr. O'Bannon had been all his life and he looked for a plot somewhere to dig, plant and watch grow. That plot turned out to be the long-idle garden spot next door, the same his father, John W. O'Bannon, had worked 30 years previous. Mr. O'Bannon had the soil turned over, well manured from his son's stables, harrowed and in no time was furnishing his sons and daughters, as well as this compiler's mother, all the vegetables they could use. His garden became a show place and he became the sage of gardening in the town of Marshall. This compiler has a picture of Mr. O'Bannon taken in his row of cabbages, any one of which would have filled a bushel basket! And the succession of "green thumbs" working that garden was not to end with Mr. O'Bannon — after his death, J. Norris O'Bannon, continued tilling the little patch and furnishing half the town with vegetables — the pride of his leisure time (other than his race horses) from the hardware business. When this compiler offered his home for sale, the O'Bannons purchased it — saving a portion of the garden spot for themselves before selling the remainder. In all those years, no one ever had better neighbors than the O'Bannons!

ISSUE (O'BANNON):

+ 420.   Dora[8], b 28 May 1907; d: 14 Nov. 1990
+ 421.   James T.[8], b: 1910; d: 26 Dec. 1976
+ 422.   Elmer Ashley[8], b: 1911
+ 423.   John Norris[8], b: 3 March 1914; d: 27 Nov. 1986
+ 424.   Virginia Josephine[8], b: 28 Nov. 1916; d: 22 July 1978
+ 425.   Paul[8]
+ 426.   Edward A.[8]
+ 427.   Bernie Lee[8]

358. HARRY LEE[7] O'BANNON (John Willis[6]) married Anna (or Annie) Wines. She was born in 1890, a dau. of Richard and Nannie Wines of Delaplane, VA. She was a member of Cool Spring Methodist Church. Mr. O'Bannon died 14 July 1960. They are buried at Ivy Hill Cemetery, Upperville, VA.

ISSUE (O'BANNON):

428.   Kitty[8], m: _____ Johnson
429.   George Thomas[8], b: 1918; d: 18 June 1971; m: _____ Issue: 1) John G.[9] and 2) Jean Herman[9]. Buried at Ivy Hill Cemetery.
430.   Richard Lee[8]

361. CECIL CORBIN[7] O'BANNON (Corbin M. L.[6], Enoch W.[5]) born 4 Nov. 1888; d: 7 Jan. 1967. Mr. O'Bannon was born at Dover, Loudoun Co., VA. In 1942 he moved to Chantilly from Manassas. A retired carpenter, he was a life member of the Chantilly Fire Department. He married Jeannette Virginia Melton, b: 11 Oct. 1890 in Fauquier County, the dau. of James and Rebecca Melton. She died 6 July 1965. They are buried at Columbia Gardens Cemetery, Arlington, VA.

ISSUE (O'BANNON):

431.   Nadine Virginia[8], b: 30 Apr. 1911; m: Charles E. Olinger, Jr., b: 2 Feb. 1910; d: 16 July 1980. He is buried at the Marshall Cemetery. Mrs. Olinger lives in Marshall where she is active in the Piedmont Chapter, U.D.C. and in both the Orlean and Marshall Baptist Churches.
432.   Kathleen Eloise[8], b: 19 Dec. 1913; d: 20 Apr. 1975; m: _____ Riley.
433.   Helen[8], m: Wm. W. Davis, of Kingston, Md. She d: 8 Aug. 1977.
434.   Evelyn Lee[8], b: 1 Feb. 1918; d: 30 June 1984
+ 435.   Cecil M.[8], b: 26 Nov. 1920
436.   Edgar Warren[8], b: 10 June 1923; d: 14 May 1924
437.   Earl F.[8], d: 1989; m: Issue: 1) Cynthia Sue[9] O'Bannon
438.   Kenneth R.[8]

EIGHTH GENERATION

371. JOHN MAURICE[8] O'BANNON, II, (J. Hill[7], Walter[6], John Maurice[5], Bryant[4], William[3], John[2], Bryan[1]), born 4 July 1923; m: 30 Nov. 1946, Louise Menefee Rudasill, daughter of Luther Rudasill, b: 12 Jan. 1925. The O'Bannons live in Woodville, VA. and Mr. O'Bannon owns and operates the Sperryville Emporium. The Emporium is located in the old Sperryville High School building.

ISSUE (O'BANNON):

+ 439.   John Maurice[9], III, b: 14 Feb. 1948
+ 440.   Robert Hill[9], b: 24 Feb. 1949
   441.   Elizabeth Catherine[9], b: 24 Aug. 1951
   442.   Martha Louise[9], b: 6 June 1953

372. MARTHA WALLACE[8] BARBER (Lilly[7], Walter[6]) born 3 Dec. 1916; m: 6 October 1934, Dr. Alfred Ringgold Armstrong, Professor at the College of William and Mary, Williamsburg, VA. The compiler is indebted to Mrs. Armstrong for sharing O'Bannon notes collected by her late mother, Lilly (O'Bannon) Barber.

ISSUE (ARMSTRONG):

443.   Robert Miller[9], b: 22 July 1938
444.   Alfred Barber[9]

373. SILAS LILLARD[8] O'BANNON (Chas. Wm.[7], Eggborn B.[6]) born 10 April 1901; died 16 Jan. 1982. He m: (1st) Mary Early, April 1923, divorced and m: (2nd) Mary Virginia Smith, 16 April 1942. Mr. O'Bannon was born near Boston, Culpeper Co., VA. He worked for the Virginia Highway Department for many years and after his second marriage moved, in 1944, to their home near Warrenton. He was a member of the Phoenix Odd Fellows Lodge in Culpeper, the Amissville Ruritan Club and served as a Deacon of the Amissville Baptist Church. In the Ruritan Club he answered to the nickname, "Governor of the Free State."

ISSUE (O'BANNON) - First marriage:

445.   Peggy Lou[9], b: 23 Nov. 1925, m: Peter Norris. Issue: 1) William[10] Norris
446.   William Albert[9], b: 16 Dec. 1930

377. ALEXANDER THOMAS[8] O'BANNON (Chas. Wm.[7], Eggborn B.[6]) m: Doris Virginia Button. Known as Sandy Thomas O'Bannon, he pre-deceased his wife who died in Sept. 1976. She was the dau. of Warren P. and Lillie Humphries Button of Culpeper County.

ISSUE (O'BANNON):

447.   Thomas Powell[9]

378. LAURA MARGARET[8] O'BANNON (Chas. Wm.[7]) born 10 Jan. 1923, m: 30 July 1941, Carter Almond Saunders, b: 3 Jan. 1919; d: 15 Jan. 1977.

ISSUE (SAUNDERS):

448.   Mildred Olga[9], b: 7 Jan. 1942
449.   Carter Almond[9], Jr., b: 11 Jan. 1944
450.   William Lamonte[9], b: 7 Jan. 1948

379. EMILY BRADFORD[8] O'BANNON (Chas. Wm.[7]) born 5 Nov. 1925; m: Charles Goodwyn Harris, 13 Feb. 1948. He was born 24 August 1914.

ISSUE (HARRIS):

451.   Caroline Lanetta[9], b: 7 Dec. 1949
452.   Mary Goodwin[9], b: 10 April 1953
453.   Elizabeth Bradford[9], b: 15 Aug. 1957

393. BETTY THOMAS[8] O'BANNON (Richard H. L.[7], Eggborn B.[6]) born 20 June 1932; m: Ralph Borden Culp, 31 March 1956. He was born 13 Nov. 1929. The Culps live in Denton, Texas where he is a Professor at North Texas State University. The compiler owes a debt of gratitude to Betty for sharing with me many O'Bannon family charts. Betty grew up in Falls Church and we had many reminiscences to share when I visited her in her mother's home in Culpeper in the hot, dry summer of 1991. She was leaving Falls Church just about the same time I was arriving to teach school at her alma mater, Falls Church High School.

ISSUE (CULP):

454.   Helen Borden[9], b: 2 Jan. 1961
455.   Elizabeth Winter[9], b: 9 March 1963
456.   Richard Bertram[9], b: 19 July 1964
457.   Jeffrey O'Bannon[9], b: 20 Feb. 1967

394. RICHARD LEE[8] O'BANNON (Richard H. L.[7], Eggborn B.[6]) born 14 October 1936. He married Sallie Gilliard. They live in Springfield, VA.

ISSUE (O'BANNON):

458. Tracy Lynn[9], b: 6 Jan. 1966
459. Michelle Lee[9], b: 5 July 1969

395. CLAUDE AARON[8] O'BANNON (Ernest W.[7], John Willis[6]) born 11 Aug. 1896; d: 5 May 1964. He married, 1929, Annie Kines of Hume, VA. He represented the State Farm Mutual Insurance for 27 years prior to his death. He was a member of the Hume Baptist Church, where he was a Deacon and president of the Brotherhood. He was also a member of Charity Lodge No. 27, I.O.O.F., Warrenton. He is buried at Leeds Cemetery, Hume, VA. No issue.

398. EMMA ELIZABETH[8] PEARSON (Florence S.[7], John Willis[6]) married 1 Dec. 1920, George Huffman Russell. Mrs. Russell taught school in Fauquier County until her marriage and for 60 years lived in Arlington, VA. The Russells are buried at Columbia Gardens Cemetery, Arlington.

ISSUE (RUSSELL):

460. Frances[9], m: _____ Dunlap. Lives at Myrtle Beach,S.C.
461. Robert W.[9]
462. Donald P.[9], d: by 1987
463. George H.[9], Jr., d: by 1987

399. EVA JOSEPHINE[8] PEARSON (Florence S.[7], John Willis[6]) born 18 Feb. 1897; d: 6 June 1982; m: Ollie Baxley Poe, 28 Jan. 1914. He was born 13 July 1886 and died 20 July 1966. Mrs. Poe was a member of Battle Run Primitive Baptist Church — her pastor wrote "she was a faithful member and her smiles are greatly missed in our church, which she loved so much. She was loved by the church and by all who knew her."

ISSUE (POE):

464. Edmund Guy[9], b: Jan. 1915; d: July 1915
465. Hazel Elizabeth[9], b: 1916; m: Ulysses Dickens Sudduth. He died 1972. Issue: 1) Linda Leigh[10]; 2) U. D., Jr.[10] (Chip), m: Elizabeth Muirhead; 3) Barry Anderson[10], m: Linda Gattis (div.), m: (2nd) Francine Summa.
466. James Everett[9], b: 1918; m: Dorothy Stultz. Issue: 1) Baxley[10] Poe; 2) Margaret Ann[10] Poe.
467. Melvin Morrison[9], b: 1920, m: Jane Carter (div.); m: (2) Margaret _____
468. Eleanor Beatrice[9], m: Charles Harvey, d: 1990
469. Delia Ann[9], m: Jack Wines, they have 4 children.
470. Roger William[9], m: Nannie Cameron. Issue: 1) Ross[10] 2) Clydetta[10]

471. Jeannette Myree[9], m: Ralph Lawler. She died 21 Nov. 1976; Ralph is also deceased. Issue: 1) Diana[10]; 2: Peggy[10]; 3) Stuart[10]; 4) Ollie Joe[10]. Jeannette and Ralph were members of the Orlean Baptist Church and are buried in the Orlean Cemetery.

472. Albert Ollie[9], m: Helen Cameron (div.); m: (2) Jackie _____. Issue (1st m:) 1) Steve[10]; 2) Larry[10].

473. Thomas Leon[9], b: 1934; m: Sandra Robinson. Issue: 1) Darrell[10]; 2) Kimberly[10]

474. Joyce Gale[9], b: 1938; m: Carlin Mills. Issue: 1) Wesley[10]; 2) Sheryl[10]; 3) Brett[10].

400. ADA VIRGINIA[8] PEARSON (Florence S.[7], John Willis[6]) m: Charles Dean, 16 Nov. 1922. They are both deceased.

ISSUE (DEAN):

475. Marian[9], m: John Lee
476. Patricia Ann[9], m: Scott Cadwallader
477. Michael[9]
478. Bernie[9], m: Ann _____

402. WALTER WILLIAM[8] PEARSON (Florence S.[7], John Willis[6]) m: (1) Myrtle Pearson, (div.); m: (2) Caroline Kirby.

404. RENA MARIE[8] PEARSON (Florence S.[7]) m: (1) Edward Hailer, 15 May 1928; m: (2) Augustus Meyer, 15 July 1961.

ISSUE (HAILER):

479. Beverly[9]
480. James Edward[9]
481. Mary Catherine[9]
482. Billie Mae[9]

406. ALMA BEATRICE[8] PEARSON (Florence S.[7], John Willis[6]) born 4 March 1912; d: 27 Sept. 1990; m: 18 June 1932, Wilbur Robinson. Mrs. Robinson was a member of the Warrenton Presbyterian Church. She and Mr. Robinson are buried in the Warrenton Cemetery.

ISSUE (ROBINSON):

483. Jane Parker[9], m: Charles Brown. Issue: 1) Steve[10], 2) Stuart[10]; 3) Christopher C.[10] Brown.

407. SUSIE GERTRUDE[8] PEARSON (Florence S.[7]) m: 8 August 1932, James Coflin. Both are deceased.

ISSUE (COFLIN):

484. Wallace[9]
485. Harriet Serepta[9]

420. DORA[8] O'BANNON (James Keith[7], John Willis[6]) married Charles Kirby. Mrs. Kirby was a member of Bethel United Methodist Church, Bethel, Fauquier Co., VA. Mr. and Mrs. Kirby are buried at the Warrenton Cemetery.

ISSUE (KIRBY):

486. Dorothy K.[9], m: Stanley Soaper, Annandale, VA.
487. Betty K.[9], m: _____ Horton
488. Haldeen Marie[9], m: 11 Aug. 1962, Thomas M. Wilson, Jr.

421. JAMES T.[8] O'BANNON (James Keith[7]) married Anna Grimes. Mr. O'Bannon worked on a farm at Marshall until 1941 when he moved to Long Green (Md.) farm of H. C. Jennifer "and first began to work with horses. In 1960 he removed to Sagamore Farms, the Baltimore County estate of Alfred G. Vanderbilt, the former president of the Maryland Jockey Club. He was the brood mare manager at Sagamore Farms and was a member of the Professional Horsemen's Association and Dover Methodist Church. Mr. O'Bannon died 26 Dec. 1976 in Carroll County, Md. and is buried at Wilson Methodist Cemetery, Long Green Valley, Md.

ISSUE (O'BANNON):

489. Charles Keith[9]

422. ELMER ASHLEY[8] O'BANNON (James Keith[7]) born 19 Nov. 1911; m: Rachel Fair, b: 20 Sept. 1917. Mr. O'Bannon is a member of the Marshall Baptist Church and Mrs. O'Bannon is a member of The Plains Baptist Church. They live in Marshall, VA.

ISSUE (O'BANNON):

+ 490. Elmer Ashley, Jr.[9], b: 11 Nov. 1935
  491. B. Joyce[9], b: 8 Oct. 1940

423. JOHN NORRIS[8] O'BANNON (James Keith[7], John Willis[6], Enoch W.[5], Enoch[4], Samuel[3], John[2], Bryan[1]) was born 3 March 1914, at "Egypt Farm" near Marshall. He married Lou Bayly Berry, dau. of Charles Temple and Kate (Strother) Berry of Fauquier. He and his wife bought the Marshall Hardware Co. in January 1946 from L. I. Poe. First located in the old Odd Fellows Building, the business was moved across the street to its present location erected by the O'Bannons. The business was incorporated in 1986 with John N. O'Bannon, Jr. as president, Mr. O'Bannon as vice-president and Mrs. O'Bannon as secretary-treasurer. Mr. O'Bannon, who fought a long battle with cancer, continued to work in the store until a few weeks before his death. He always put his customers first in his business and was unfailingly helpful in dealing with his patrons. His outside activities included his garden and his thoroughbred race horses. Mr. O'Bannon was one of the organizers and a charter member of the Marshall Volunteer Fire Department. He helped organize the original Marshall Sanitary Company and was a director of the Marshall National Bank and Trust Co. for 26 years. His funeral service was held at the Marshall Baptist Church, with burial at Leeds Cemetery, Markham. In his personal life Mr. O'Bannon was known for his honesty in all dealings, straight-forward and candid. He was a good neighbor, who with his wife, was (and she is) always ready to lend a hand and go the extra mile.

ISSUE (O'BANNON):

+ 492.   John Norris, Jr.[9]
  493.   Infant son.

424. VIRGINIA JOSEPHINE[8] O'BANNON (James Keith[7]) was born at Marshall, VA. and died, 1978, in Fairfax, VA. She was a member of the Unison United Methodist Church. She m: Charles Cannon Cassell, Sr. Mrs. Cassell was buried at Ebenezer Cemetery, near Round Hill, VA.

ISSUE (CASSELL):

494.   Charles Cannon, Jr.[9]
495.   Joseph Keith[9]

425. PAUL[8] O'BANNON (James Keith[7]) m: Lydia E. Entzian. They live in Edgewater, Maryland.

ISSUE (O'BANNON):

496.   Kenneth[9], b: 31 Oct. 1948; m: Linda Hill. Kenneth is a 1970 graduate of the U. S. Naval Academy, Annapolis, and is now (1991) a Commander in the U. S. Navy. Kenneth and his wife were present at the commissioning of the U.S.S. O'BANNON on 15 Dec. 1980 at the Ingalls Shipbuilding Division, Pascagoula, Miss. Knowing the interest of this compiler in Lt. Presley N. O'Bannon, for whom the ship was named (the third to bear his name), secured a medal struck for the occasion and printed material.
497.   Joan[9], b: 14 Feb. 1950; m: Robert Timko

498. Janet[9], b: 4 Apr. 1956, m: George Moses

426. EDWARD A.[8] O'BANNON (James Keith[7]) married Teresa Kines of Hume, Virginia. They live in Front Royal, VA.

ISSUE (O'BANNON):

499. Daniel[9]
500. William[9]

427. BERNIE LEE[8] O'BANNON (James Keith[7]) married 19 February 1954, Mary Elam of Hume, Virginia. Mr. O'Bannon has been employed by the Marshall Hardware Co. for most of his adult life. They live in Marshall, VA.

ISSUE (O'BANNON):

501. Bernie Lee, Jr.[9], b: 7 Aug. 1955; m: 28 June 1980, Lisa Lynn Watson. Issue: 1) Michael[10]; 2) Lindsay Marie[10].
502. Jeffery Norris[9], b: 5 Jan. 1959; m: Christine Wilder. Issue: 1) Adam Norris[10] O'Bannon
503. Mary Lou[9], b: 9 Jan. 1964; m: John Bobst. Issue: 1) Brandon Thomas[10] Bobst.

435. CECIL M.[8] O'BANNON (Cecil C.[7], Corbin M.L.[6], Enoch W.[5]) married Virginia E. Thompson. She was born 30 June 1916 and died 17 March 1987. She is buried at Columbia Gardens Cemetery, Arlington, VA.

ISSUE (O'BANNON):

504. Cecil C.[9], III, b: 31 Aug. 1948; d: 22 June 1972;m: Joyce A. ____. Had: 1) Patrick Michael[10] and 2) Wendy Sue[10].
505. Dolores[9]
506. Donna[9]
507. Charles P.[9]

NINTH GENERATION

439. JOHN MAURICE[9] O'BANNON, III (J. Maurice[8], J. Hill[7], Walter[6], John Maurice[5], Bryant[4], William[3], John[2], Bryan[1]) Dr. O'Bannon graduated from the Medical College of Virginia in Richmond, VA., where he lives and practices his profession. He married 27 June 1971, in Richmond, Virginia, Patricia Anne Steinmetz, daughter of Mr. and Mrs. Granville Harding Steinmetz of Richmond.

ISSUE (O'BANNON):

508.   John Harding[10], b: 31 July 1974, called "Jack"
509.   Virginia Louise[10], b: 20 August 1976, called "Ginny"
510.   Andrew Hill[10], b: 7 December 1979

440. ROBERT HILL[9] O'BANNON (J. Maurice[8]) was educated at Fork Union Military Academy and after a brief college career, joined the U. S. Marine Corps and served in Vietnam. He m: (1st), 27 March 1956, Susan Ann Payne, divorced, and married (2nd) 2 Oct. 1976, Polly Ann Crossman, daughter of Mr. and Mrs. William K. Crossman of Rapidan, VA. They live in Culpeper, VA. where Mr. O'Bannon is employed by the C & P Telephone Company of Virginia.

ISSUE (O'BANNON):

511.   Jason Matthew[10], b: 11 December 1980
512.   Kathie Ann[10], b: 3 October 1985

490. ELMER ASHLEY[9] O'BANNON, JR. (Elmer A.[8], James Keith[7]) married 17 November 1956, at Marshall Baptist Church, Marshall, VA., Helen Z. Chappelear, daughter of L. Clayton and Bertha (Hackley) Chappelear. Following their divorce, Mr. O'Bannon married (2nd) Barbara Lillard.

ISSUE (O'BANNON): (First Marriage):

513.   Gareth Alan[10], b: 15 Feb. 1961, in Arlington, VA., m: 27 Dec. 1983, Marshall, VA., Flora A. Garvey, dau. of Mr. and Mrs. Richard E. Garvey, Sr. of Downingtown, PA. Mr. O'Bannon is an officer in the U. S. Army and served in Desert Storm, 1991.
514.   Timothy Darien[10], b: 22 Nov. 1962, Fairfax, VA.

492. JOHN NORRIS[9] O'BANNON, JR. (J. Norris[8], James Keith[7], John Willis[6], Enoch W.[5], Enoch[4], Samuel[3], John[2], Bryan[1]) attended Woodberry Forest School in Orange County, VA and graduated from the University of North Carolina. At both school and university, Mr. O'Bannon excelled in sports. On 11 August 1961, while still a student at U.N.C., he married Suzanne Taylor, daughter of Mr. and Mrs. J.R. Taylor, of North Carolina. This marriage ended in divorce and Mr.

O'Bannon married (2nd), Sharon Lee Rich, daughter of Mr. and Mrs. David H. Rich, Sr. of Warrenton, VA. Mr. and Mrs. O'Bannon live in Marshall, VA. where he is co-owner of the Marshall Hardware Co., Inc.

ISSUE (O'BANNON):

515.   LuAnne[10]
516.   Tracye Taylor[10], b: 3 January 1968

ISSUE (2nd Marriage):

517.   John Norris[10] III,

Other books by John K. Gott:

An Historical Vignette of Oak Hill, Fauquier County: Home of John Marshall,
Chief Justice of the United States and Native Son of Fauquier County
T. Triplett Russell and John K. Gott

CD: Fauquier County, Virginia Court Records, 1776-1782

CD: Fauquier County, Virginia Deeds, 1759-1785, Volumes 1 and 2

CD: Fauquier County, Virginia Guardian Bonds, 1759-1871

CD: Fauquier County, Virginia Marriage Bonds, 1759-1854 and Marriage Returns, 1785-1848

CD: Fauquier County, Virginia

Fauquier County, Virginia Court Records, 1776-1782

Fauquier County in the Revolution
T. Triplett Russell and John K. Gott

Fauquier County, Virginia Deed Abstracts, 1779-1785

Fauquier County, Virginia Guardian Bonds, 1759-1871

Fauquier County, Virginia Deeds, 1759-1778

Fauquier County, Virginia Deeds, 1778-1785

Fauquier County, Virginia: Marriage Bonds (1759-1854), and Marriage Returns (1785-1848)

One Hundred Years of Cochran Lodge, 1899-1999: Cochran Lodge No. 271, A.F. & A.M., The Plains, Virginia

The Years of Anguish: Fauquier County, Virginia, 1861-1865
Emily G. Ramey and John K. Gott

Valiant Virginian: Story of Presley Neville O'Bannon, 1776-1850, to Which is Added the O'Bannon Family
Trudy J. Sundberg and John K. Gott

www.ingramcontent.com/pod-product-compliance
Lightning Source LLC
Chambersburg PA
CBHW080333270326
41927CB00014B/3198